THE SHAAR PRESS

THE JUDAICA IMPRINT
FOR THOUGHTFUL PEOPLE

A guide to the
first year of marriage …
and beyond

THE
SHAAR
PRESS

to
We

SHIFRAH DEVORAH WITT

Published by **SHAAR PRESS**
Distributed by MESORAH PUBLICATIONS, LTD.
4401 Second Avenue / Brooklyn, N.Y 11232 / (718) 921-9000

Distributed in Israel by SIFRIATI / A. GITLER
Moshav Magshimim / Israel

Distributed in Europe by LEHMANNS
Unit E, Viking Business Park, Rolling Mill Road / Jarrow, Tyne and Wear, NE32 3DP/ England

Distributed in Australia and New Zealand by GOLDS WORLD OF JUDAICA
3-13 William Street / Balaclava, Melbourne 3183 / Victoria Australia

Distributed in South Africa by KOLLEL BOOKSHOP
Northfield Centre / 17 Northfield Avenue / Glenhazel 2192, Johannesburg, South Africa

ISBN 10: 1-4226-1598-7 / ISBN 13: 978-1-4226-1598-0

Printed in the United States of America
Custom bound by Sefercraft, Inc. / 4401 Second Avenue / Brooklyn N.Y. 11232

For my husband,
Yedidya:

Your commitment to working on yourself
and our marriage is remarkable.
You are amazing.

And to our children,

Menachem Mendel,
Noam Elimelech,
and our new daughter, Bracha.

I am endlessly grateful for each of you
and the joy you bring to my life.
May you all grow to Torah, chuppah,
and ma'asim tovim, and each be blessed
to build your own bayis ne'eman
in the right time with the right one.

Table Of Contents

Part 1

Making the Shift from Me to We

Part 2

Advice From Women Who Know

Part 3

Let's Talk About It...

Acknowledgments

There are so many people who made this book possible, and I want to acknowledge and thank them all. Thank you to my mom, Zipporah Malka Heller, who encouraged me, worked countless hours on the initial edit of this book, and babysat while I worked on this manuscript.

Thank you to Miriam Zakon, the warmest and kindest of editors, and to Shmuel Blitz, as well as everyone else at Shaar Press who made this manuscript a book and believed in the importance of its message.

Thanks to Suri Brand, who edited this book, and Chaya Baila Gavant, who proofread. You can't imagine how happy I am to work with both of you on this project. And thanks to Jenny Weisberg, Leah Kotkes, Esther Heller, Tamar Ansh, and Sarah Shapiro, who have all inspired me in different ways.

Thanks to the amazing women who contributed to this book, both their wisdom and their writing. I learned so much from each of you. May you be blessed with success in your marriages and everything you do.

And finally, thank you to my new baby, Bracha. It was your imminent arrival that pushed me to finish this book and share it with the world.

Author's Note

This book is my gift to every *kallah* at every age and stage in life. There is nothing as precious as building a *bayis ne'eman b'Yisrael*, a Jewish family. With that in mind, I have compiled advice, stories, tips, and guidelines to help you build the best marriage you can from the first year of marriage on.

My husband's and my first year of marriage was a wonderful time of learning and growth, filled with misunderstandings, funny stories, and a few moments I wish I could do over, but mainly lots of goodwill and a commitment to building a strong foundation for our *bayis ne'eman*.

For us, *baruch Hashem*, our *shanah rishonah* is already ten years behind us. Still, I think of the stories I lived, heard, and saw that year, plus the stories people have come to me with since then. I've heard lots of women's stories and been asked many questions on the topic of the first year of marriage as friends have shared their lives with me. I have often thought,

I wish there were something I could offer to help make the adjustment of shanah rishonah sweeter.

This book is my answer. I hope it inspires you to grow and helps you along your path to creating the best marriage possible.

Note: All the authors whose names are marked with an asterisk are using pen names.

Introduction

Mazel tov! You're a *kallah*. With Hashem's help, the next year is going to be the most magically wonderful year of your life. The long-awaited and mysterious *shanah rishonah* is finally here. This is your chance to build the home you have always dreamed of. From decorating your first apartment to making dinner, from deciding if you'll be working to the country and city in which you should start your journey together, this year is about making choices and deciding how you'll lay the foundation for your *bayis ne'eman b'Yisrael*.

The first year of marriage is also filled with lots of questions and lots of learning. In the coming months, you'll learn new things about yourself and about your husband. This book is designed to help you through the learning process I like to call "the journey of *shanah rishonah*." It's a special year filled with self-discovery and lots of new experiences.

When I was a *kallah*, I was amazed at the amount of attention I got. People I barely knew — friends of my future husband's family — were offering to take me, the "*kallah*," to lunch. Others offered to help out with the wedding in any way they could. I was suddenly the focus of every conversation I entered, from the moment I got engaged until the *sheva berachos* were over, though I never asked for it. I was the center of attention.

After lots of anticipation, my wedding day finally came. I was blessed to marry my wonderful husband, and I felt Hashem's kindness more intensely than I ever had in my life. A week of incredible *sheva berachos* later, I was both elated and exhausted. I couldn't wait for things to settle down. I was excited to get into real life and make the move from being a bride to becoming a wife.

My real life, the one I had been waiting for, was about to begin. Much to my surprise, about a month into my married life, the excitement and attention I'd gotten used to were abruptly over.

Like most new brides, the very beginning of our marriage was filled with the excitement of opening wedding presents, setting up the apartment, and getting used to covering my hair. Since we were in Israel, I had a few extra things to deal with, including figuring out what *hechsheirim* were in accordance with our standards of kashrus and which shul was a good fit.

We were now living in Jerusalem, where my husband was a native. I was a long way from home and felt a little lost. Truth be told, I was confused about how to do just about anything in this new city and culture. I had lots of questions and had absolutely no clue where to find the answers.

My husband left the house at 5 a.m. and was learning until about 8 p.m., when he returned home exhausted. I knew only a handful of people, and everything I was comfortable with back home was no longer my reality. At home, I'd had a great job and a community of friends and family. If I was ever bored,

I simply picked up the phone and within minutes I had plans. Now everything was different. And I realized how far away I felt from my old life.

There is a custom to eat with families and friends the first year of marriage, so you can learn from more established couples. So we attempted to socialize by going away for Shabbos.

One Shabbos, I was standing in the kitchen of my hostess when a neighbor of hers dropped by for a late Shabbos afternoon chat. I was introduced as the new *kallah*. The friend plunged into a long story about how hard her *shanah rishonah* was and continued to tell me how hard it was to be married and that I shouldn't worry if I was finding it difficult. She suggested therapy if things weren't going well. I thought she was strange and excused myself as politely as possible.

A few Shabbosos later a similar experience happened, this time at a different friend's house. The conversation also turned to how challenging *shanah rishonah* was. The conclusion was that I shouldn't be embarrassed if things were hard: I should feel free to ask for help.

The irony of both of these experiences was that I was perfectly happy with my husband. Though it was taking me a bit of time to adjust to living in a foreign country, otherwise we were having a beautiful *shanah rishonah*.

I started to get nervous. Did this mean something was wrong with us? Was I just lucky that the first few months had gone so smoothly? Did this mean *shanah rishonah* was going to be all right but I should be afraid of *shanah sheniyah*, the second year of marriage?

After much consideration, I realized three things: (1) I was really lucky I had married a wonderful man and we were doing well; (2) it isn't infrequent to have a really difficult first year of marriage, hence the horror stories in the Shabbos kitchens; and (3) it would be really nice if there was something out there to make the transition that much easier.

There is no gift more precious for your future children than being a living example of a healthy Jewish marriage. May this book help you on your journey to creating that marriage. Mazel tov, *kallah*, to growth, commitment, and becoming the best you can be in the process.

Part 1

Making the Shift from Me to We

Chapter 1

Dreaming of Shanah Rishonah: Expectations, Expectations, Expectations!

Let's be honest: the average Jewish girl spends a fair part of her life before marriage dreaming about what her life will be like after marriage. It's natural. We're women. We look to the future with a sense of hope, joy, and expectation. Why wouldn't we?

Before we ever started dating, we were often advised to think about the kind of home we want to have. Will we choose a partner who is in learning, working, or a combination of both? Do we see ourselves living in the city, the suburbs, or a different country like Eretz Yisrael? On a certain level, we are not only advised to have expectations before marriage, we are encouraged to develop them. The question becomes, What are healthy expectations and what are the expectations we need to learn to let go?

In life, when a person is suffering, if you trace the root of his pain to its source, frequently the suffering stems from expectations that are not being fulfilled. *We should have more money. He/she should be kinder. I should be further along with my career by now. I should be married by now. We should have children by now. How could things have turned out like this? This isn't what I planned for. This isn't what I expected.*

But if you ask yourself, *What would my life be like without this expectation,* oftentimes the answer comes back, *A lot happier.* Although it's natural to have expectations, one must strive to decipher which are the healthy ones and which are the ones that are making us miserable. Are our expectations worth what they are costing us? Are they realistic and fair to ask of our partners? Are our expectations realistic and fair to ask of ourselves?

As new *kallah*s, the goal is to create an environment in our homes that allows them to run as smoothly as possible, to fill them with love and infuse them with an air of peace and joy. Some expectations will foster those ideals; others will hinder them. The task is to decide which are the expectations in life and marriage that will push us toward our goals and bring us joy and which are the expectations we need to let go of to achieve the *bayis ne'eman b'Yisrael* we are all striving to create.

Think about where you are in your life right now. Which expectations are you holding on to? Which expectations are helping you push forward and grow? Which expectations are hurting you because they are unrealistic, out of your reach at the moment or simply not being met? Would you be happier if you let go of them?

There are few feelings worse than knowing you are disappointing someone you love, but sometimes disappointing yourself can be equally, if not more, devastating. How often in life are we encouraged to clarify and explore our expectations on a subject? When you get engaged, no one asks you what your mission statement is for your marriage. If anyone ever asked Jewish women what their mission statement was, we would all probably allow the same sentence to roll off our collective tongues: *To build a bayis ne'eman b'Yisrael, of course.*

The question is, what does that mean to you? What are your expectations for how that home should be built, and, equally important, what are your husband's expectations? Although these may seem like simple questions, often we don't realize just how many expectations we've already set up in our mind's eye, whether we've expressed them or not.

Recently I interviewed a new *kallah*. I asked her, "Is marriage anything like you expected?"

She replied, "It is more wonderful and at times more frustrating than I thought possible."

Then I asked, "Is there anything you expected in marriage that isn't happening?"

"Yes," she replied. "I expected Shabbos flowers. Lots and lots of Shabbos flowers."

It was interesting to see how, *baruch Hashem*, most aspects of this *kallah*'s life were going beautifully, but this one thing affected her overall *simchah*. I am not saying she is wrong for her feelings; on the contrary, I am saying how simple it would be to fix, if only each party's expectations were made clear.

Many years before I was married, I visited a friend in California. In their home, they had a beautiful collage. When I went to take a close look, I realized it had words on it. I inquired about it, and my friend told me it was their "commitment statement."

I loved the idea and carried it with me. How beautiful to put down in writing what you are committed to in your marriage. I decided I would definitely make a similar collage one day.

By the time I was married, I had forgotten all about the idea of a commitment statement or mission statement in marriage. But now that I think about it, my husband and I should really try this. The idea of clarifying both commitments and expectations to oneself and one's spouse can help set a couple up to succeed in a way chance and luck will never offer.

I'm embarrassed to admit it, but I feel I would be remiss in not sharing a personal story of expectations in my own life. *Baruch Hashem*, I feel blessed to have a wonderful husband who is kind, generous, and very polite. It's not in his nature to criticize. After six and a half years of marriage, more as an accident than a direct request, my husband finally let it slip that he found it difficult to come home on Friday night and see the table not set.

I had absolutely no idea this was an issue for him. For years I have cooked ridiculously elaborate Shabbos meals, from seven-course Japanese meals to Moroccan, Mexican, and Thai extravaganzas. By the time I'd light the candles, I could barely stand up. I had always given myself time between lighting and my husband's arrival at home after shul to rest a little and get off my feet. Then I got the salad course together, which always seemed to take a long time.

Apparently his mother always made a beautiful but much simpler Shabbos meal and always set the table at noon. When his father came in from shul, he could always sit down at the table and start Kiddush immediately. It really bothered my husband that I was nowhere near ready for Kiddush when he walked in the door from shul.

I was clueless. I simply had no idea. I changed my practice immediately and started setting the table as early as possible on Friday. It is my greatest pleasure to make my husband happy. If only I had known his expectation earlier in our lives together, how much *simchah* I could have added to our Shabbosos instead of causing unknown stress.

Marriage and life are often like this. Simple solutions often exist for our problems. But if we don't clarify our expectations, we don't know there are even issues to work on.

Consider making three lists:

1. Your expectations for yourself.
2. Your expectations for your husband's role in your marriage.
3. Your expectations for your marriage in general.

   If your husband is comfortable with this activity, have him make the same lists. Make time to sit down and compare your lists. If you don't have a realistic vision of where you see your relationship going, it will be a lot harder to get there. Clarity will only make things easier.

The following stories are from different *kallah*s and illustrate their expectations in marriage. Some decided to keep their expectations, while others decided a modification was in order.

Redefining Our Phone

● *Sarah Rachel Martin*

I had heard about the adjustments of shanah rishonah. Anyone who was honest would admit that there are a lot of lessons, surprises, and hard work that hide behind the glorious glamour leading to the first anniversary. My friends and I joked about all the funny stories, like fighting over whether to roll the toothpaste tube or making the same fish recipe for supper seven times before finally realizing that your husband hated the taste of fish. We laughed and talked and assumed we'd all have something funny to add to the repertoire of stories. Still, I never dreamed of the differences that we'd notice so blatantly.

One night we were sitting down to supper together. I was excited to have my husband home from kollel after spending a whole day alone in our new home. I didn't really know anyone yet, and even my gourmet supper could only entertain me for a chunk of the long day while my husband was learning. So after the shopping, cooking, and cleaning, not to mention all the thought that went into the stuffed spinach pizza that I had prepared for him, you can only imagine how proud I was when we sat down at the simple but beautifully set table.

Of course, I only found out later that he hates spinach, doesn't want the calories of a double crust, and would rather not wash at supper. But that wasn't the problem. He politely washed and began to eat my delectable dinner.

"Wow, this is fancy." Now that I know him better, I realize what he was really thinking: *Pareve enough. I didn't compliment the food itself, but she'll know I appreciate the effort. I can't tell her I really don't like it.*

"Thank you!" I basked in his acknowledgment, especially when he asked for a second helping.

"How was your day? It must be a little boring for you."

"A little." I smiled sheepishly. "Maybe I'll meet some people at the upcoming neighborhood Nshei event. I could use some company while you're away during the day. How was your day?"

"Baruch Hashem, settling into yeshivah. I mean, I've been in this yeshivah before, so it's not as if I'm starting from scratch like you. It's really admirable that you agreed to come all the way to Israel."

"I'm thrilled to be here but —"

I never got to finish my sentence because the phone interrupted me. Not that I was disturbed by the ring of the phone — I barely noticed it, being so engrossed in our discussion — but my husband heard it. And he got up to answer it.

How rude, I brooded. Is this how much he values me? The phone rings and he jumps to answer as if there's some emergency. Who could be so important? We're not waiting for a phone call. I should have priority over anyone else now. This is not a good way to start.

I listened as he said hi to the intruding caller. It was probably a potential chavrusa or an old friend from his yeshivah days. The conversation was brief, and he even ended it especially abruptly with "My wife is waiting. We're in the middle of supper." Still, I thought this was a real injustice. Not that I'm a tough person or judgmental either, for that matter. But from the perspective of how I grew up, this was unacceptable.

———

While my husband talked on the phone, my mind drifted back a couple months. My whole family was sitting down at the supper table. In our home, supper was a family meal and it was sacred. When the phone rang, my mother was known to say, "The phone in this house is not my master. I will not be its slave." And that's how it was. The phone was used to our advantage when we wanted to use it. Well, I won't say I never wanted to use it during mealtime, but regardless, it wasn't allowed and I had to remember it wasn't my master.

At this particular meal, however, I was waiting for a phone call from my chassan. No one could debate the importance of this phone call, so I was granted permission to answer the call and leave the supper table early. Studying for tests, homework, schmoozing — none of it had its place at this hour, normally. But this was a real exception.

Dreaming of Shanah Rishonah: | 25

The phone rang and I jumped to check if it was my prized chassan. Everyone jumped with me, so shocked at the change in routine, though we had all anticipated it in advance.

"I'm so sorry," my husband said to me when he returned to the table, but I was barely listening as I bit my lip to try to hold back tears. For me, the rest of supper was spoiled. I tried to understand my husband's view based on his experience, but I just couldn't relate. My upbringing was too deeply ingrained, and though I knew I wasn't really being fair to him, I couldn't help it.

"It's fine," I mustered, but it really wasn't.

"That's just how I was raised. It's really nothing personal."

"Oh." How could it not be anything personal? I wondered as I wiped away the tears before my mascara began to run.

The first yom tov came around. We were going to be splitting the time between my parents and my in-laws. Although very excited, I was slightly anxious about moving into my in-laws' home. Though I respected them, there were many ways to do things, and it would be hard to get used to so many differences, even if they were small. Even more, it would be challenging to decide what we would incorporate in our own home from each side.

When we arrived at my in-laws' house, we were greeted by fresh take-out subway sandwiches. There were both steak and chicken cutlets to choose from. The table was set and there were a variety of drinks out as well. Isn't it nice that the meal is ready right away? I marveled. In my parents' home, supper was served very late, and I always wished I could arrive home to a hot meal. This was admirable.

"How was the flight?" my father-in-law asked.

"You must be exhausted," my mother-in-law chimed in before we could answer.

"We're so happy you're here," they said together. *"Can we get you anything else? You probably —"*

Ring, ring, ring.

"Kids, who was using the phone last?" my mother-in-law called.

"Where's the phone?" My father-in-law stood up and began to look.

"National emergency," my husband joked.

"Boys, where is the phone? Is it upstairs?"

After finally finding the portable receiver, my mother-in-law tried to answer the phone calmly. "Hi. How are you? I'm so sorry to have kept you waiting. We just couldn't find the phone. Anyway, what's doing?"

You could've kept her waiting until after supper, I thought. That's what answering machines are for. My husband was already chatting with his father, though my nerves were frazzled by the sudden interruption.

I had to control myself from really laughing because it was so comical. Now I understood exactly where my husband was coming from. No explaining could have done justice to witnessing the scene in action. It was definitely nothing personal. It was just a way of life!

Would it be our way of life? That was yet to be seen.

I'm Married — Now What?

● Rochel Boyde

I got married on August 22. Unfortunately, our apartment was not going to be ready until September 18. So for almost a month, my husband and I were wandering Jews (literally). We spent the first few days traveling from Florida, where we had our wedding, through South Carolina, where my husband is from, to D.C., where we lived. Then we moved into his company's apartment for a few weeks.

Let's be honest for a minute: "apartment" is by no means the right word for the 300-square-foot room we found ourselves living in.

We packed the place as full as we could with our belongings and stored the rest with a friend. The kitchen consisted of a sink, oven, dishwasher, and fridge. None of the appliances were kosher so we ate out a lot. (Note: That dishwasher will come back to haunt us later in this story.)

So here I was, newly married and just learning how to live with another person. And we were learning how to live with each other in a 300-square-foot room. Couple our living situation with my expectations of wifedom, and it made for some interesting situations.

See, I just knew that I would be the perfect wife. I would be the wife who always had hot meals on the table at exactly the moment my husband was hungry. I would be the wife who kept an immaculately clean home and who always looked put together. I would be the wife who never nagged her husband. I would, in fact, be the wife who has never once, in the history of mankind, existed. My parents always taught me that I could be anyone I wanted to be, and I believed them.

Now I was trying to set up a home in a, thankfully, temporary apartment. I didn't have the space or the cooking equipment necessary to welcome my husband home from work with a set table and a hot meal. But I quickly learned that deli sandwiches and chopped veggies would work. I didn't have a home to keep clean — we were literally climbing over piles of stuff with every step we took — but he was happy just to have clean clothes. I didn't have the energy to sort through boxes of stuff to find a *new outfit for each day; I quickly learned he didn't care if I wore the same pair of shoes two days in a row. And that nagging thing? Forget about it. We both nagged. It's what a 300-square-foot apartment will do to a person.*

———————

Anyone else ever dream of a fairy-tale marriage? You know the kind. Everything is perfect all the time. Except that nothing is perfect all the time. Things happen. One time I ate all the cookies in the apartment, and my husband didn't get any. Why are you surprised? I told you, nothing is perfect.

I'm pretty sure that when my husband asked me to marry him, he assumed that I would always stay exactly the same. But when we were going out, I was trying to impress him. I didn't want him to know about my chocolate addiction or my cookie-thieving ways. I didn't mind spending three hours doing my hair and makeup. Now, well, baruch Hashem for sheitels.

My husband's lifelong dream was to spend time living overseas. To that end, he had lived frugally while single in order to set aside the necessary money. I now wear his travel money on my ring finger. At first, I didn't understand; I would have been just as happy with a smaller diamond or a thinner band. Later, I came to realize the significance of his gift: he was still spending the money on a dream — just a different one. My engagement and wedding rings serve as a daily physical reminder of the commitment we made to each other under the chuppah.

The standard kesubah text states that virtually everything a wife owns is now owned by her husband. If both partners in a couple go into the marriage expecting that everything they own is also owned by the other person, then you can enter a true partnership. At least, that's how

I defend myself against allegations that I ate the last of the blueberry-oat bars, the chocolate-chip cookie bars, and the oatmeal-raisin cookies. Well, I'm sure you get the picture.

The point isn't that I don't want to impress him anymore. The point is that I already know I impress him. I impress him when I'm able to juggle a full day of work, errands, chores, and still find time at the end of the day to work on building a relationship with him. Beating him at Uno is relationship building, right?

I always expected married life to be easy. I imagined that everything would be perfect. Of course, I realized that everyone faces challenges. I just didn't think that our first big one would occur so soon after our wedding. It's ironic, really, that that first hurdle was a really small apartment. I learned that being able to face challenges together with a sense of humor makes all the difference in the world.

Remember that dishwasher I told you about? Apparently, the sink drained into the dishwasher and the dishwasher didn't drain at all. At first, my husband and I got frustrated. Then we realized that there was no reason to be frustrated with each other. And, when you really think about it, it was funny. (I try not to really think about it.) It was a story — an experience — that we shared. It was something that happened to us together. We both had the opportunity to see how the other one dealt with stress. We have different personalities. I'm much louder and a little more dramatic. He's more patient and a lot more logical. He solves problems. I make jokes. Teamwork, people, teamwork.

Here's the real deal: once you're married, you'll have bad days. You'll have days when you are tired, cranky, or sick. You'll have days during which your spouse won't be at his or her best. That's O.K. See, when you're not at your best, your spouse will lift you up. When your spouse isn't at his or her best, you'll return the favor.

I didn't understand how much our role as partners would affect our marriage. We operate in different spheres. Sure, he kills the bugs. I wash the dishes. Let me just say that I am perfectly content with this dynamic. He runs out to the store late at night when I need something. I sleep eight hours every night so I'm not cranky during the day. Trust me, it's really more for his benefit than mine.

On a serious note, we complement each other. We both do the things that we know the other would prefer not to do.

I think I expected that in our marriage I would do everything I needed to do on my own. I wanted to show off. I wanted him to be impressed. I wouldn't accept help because I wouldn't need it.

But then something happened. The more I asserted my independence, the more he asserted his. Slowly but surely, my patient and loving husband taught me that I don't need to impress him. He relied on me and, in doing so, he taught me how to rely on him. He showed me that accepting help just meant that there were two of us working toward my goals. You see, I have goals. I have enormous, time-consuming, energy-depleting goals. I have goals that I wouldn't be able to accomplish on my own. But I have a husband who is dead set on pushing every obstacle out of the way so that I can soar. I know, without a doubt, that we can accomplish anything and everything we want out of life.

Of course, I'm not the only one in this marriage with goals. My husband also has many. It's one of the things I admire most about him and one of the many reasons I married him. My husband trusts me to help him suc-

ceed. He relies on my intellect and my problem-solving skills. Sure, he depends on me to keep our fridge stocked and our apartment tidy. But, more than that, he depends on me to make our home a positive place full of laughter and joy. Most importantly, he gains strength from my unending belief that if we work hard, there is nothing out of our reach. And I am so ready to work hard so that we can make each and every one of his dreams come true.

My husband and I are best friends. We are also each other's number-one cheerleaders. But he's more than that. He's the person who will never let me fail. He'll prop me up in any way he can. It does not matter to him if he gets credit for it or not. What matters to him is that I'm happy, healthy, and able to fulfill my potential. As for me, well, I do the same for him.

There is a mishnah in Pirkei Avos in which a pious man is described as a person who says, "What's mine is yours and what's yours is yours." That should be the expectation that each of us has when we enter into marriage. Marriage isn't about ownership; it's about partnership. When we give of ourselves freely, our marriage benefits. When we serve as each other's helpmates, our bond strengthens. The best marriage advice I received, and the best I can pass on to you, is this: try your best, every day, to make each other happy.

Time Not My Own

● S. L. Weinstock*

Erev Shavuos. I was married a little over two months and about to celebrate my first yom tov in my own home. Since I was working two jobs but had erev yom tov off, I planned to cook all day erev yom tov: fleishig meals in the morning, milchig meals in the afternoon. After all, it was a long day, wasn't it?

I knew how to cook, so that was no problem, but I'd never done this entirely on my own before, which is how I found myself at 3 p.m. on erev yom tov staring at a sink full of dirty dishes, with yom tov a mere four hours away, my heart sinking to my shoes. I'd finally finished the fleishig meals, only two hours behind schedule, but how was I ever going to get everything else done before candle lighting?

My husband, totally oblivious to my plight, was at the computer in the other room, writing a complex dvar Torah to e-mail to his family. At 4 p.m., he proudly entered the kitchen to show me the fruits of his labors. I threw it a dutiful glance, pretending to be impressed as my heart pounded in the race against the clock.

By 5:30, I'd managed to get a luscious cheesecake assembled. Desperately I shoved sticky mixing bowls, measuring cups, and spoons into the spare dishpan under the sink. I'd just have to deal with the dish disaster after yom tov.

My husband went off, whistling cheerfully, to sweep the floor and polish his shoes. I slid a pan of fish into the oven and stopped to catch my breath. A glance at the clock told me it was no use — I'd never be able to make the elaborate salad and side dish I'd planned. Potato borekas with mushroom sauce? Forget it. We'd be eating an awful lot of cheesecake this yom tov.

I wish I could tell you that on motza'ei yom tov I washed all my dishes, both milchigs and fleishigs, and went to bed with a clean conscience. Alas, I had a work deadline coming up, and motza'ei yom tov found me at the computer, racing against the clock once again. Would this roller-coaster ride ever end?

It did, but not for a long time. Not until shanah risho-
nah was over, in fact. I'm a fantastically hard worker, but
up until my marriage, I'd never learned that my body has
its limits, that it isn't made for nonstop activity. Until that
point, I'd been focused on schoolwork, learning — cerebral
activities. The physical realm was just not mine. Suddenly,
I had to add housework, errands, and grocery shopping into
an already packed schedule, keeping me busy from morn-
ing until night. I didn't know how to take breaks. As a sin-
gle girl living at home, I'd never needed to. In all honesty,
the idea of taking a break never even entered my mind.

I lost weight, and my newlywed husband found it
difficult to understand why I was so tense all the time.
The sheer amount of time and energy that keeping house
required was far more than I'd ever bargained for, and I
never had a second to myself.

While I'd been very busy as a single, ultimately my
time had all been my own. To have my time taken up by
things I had no choice about — laundry, dishes, meals,
shopping — was a whole new experience. And though
my husband helped out whenever I asked him to, he was
learning all day and really had very little clue of what I
was going through. I didn't understand what I was going
through myself.

Months of frustration, strained nerves, hurt feelings,
and painfully learned lessons passed as I tried to adjust
to my new life of wifehood and housekeeping. I wish I'd
known, after I got engaged, that marriage involved a com-
plete lifestyle change. I wish I'd known that I was about
to undertake a whole new set of responsibilities — not just
to my husband but also to my home and myself. Things
that had previously been attended to by my mother had
suddenly been relegated to me. The sheer amount of work
was overwhelming.

Ten years have passed since that erev Shavuos when I found myself racing against the clock. Today I'm a lot wiser when it comes to Shabbos and yom tov preparations. My house is more or less in order; I've learned to juggle work, family, and home. But deep inside I still remember that feeling of being caught off guard and having to face a challenge that felt harder than it should have been. I expected too much of myself as a kallah, and I suffered for it.

When I meet new kallahs now, I tell them not to expect too much from themselves, to know that the beginning is an adjustment and that it's a special time you can't get back. Expectations can make or break a first year in marriage. My advice: choose yours wisely.

The Life I Thought I Wanted

●— *Chevy Klein**

To say I'd dreamt about getting married could be classified as the understatement of the century. I know it's a cliché, but it's true. I was twenty-five years old by the time my turn came around. My best friends had all married at nineteen and were already busy with three kids each, husbands, and some with careers, too.

Me, well, it just took longer. I didn't want to settle. And so far, everyone I had gone out with would have been settling, big time. I had this feeling that when I met him I would just know. So I waited and had plenty of time to dream, imagine, hope, and clarify what I wanted and what I was sure my life, and especially my marriage, would be like.

At first I started with the easy stuff. We'd live in Los Angeles, La Brea side. That's where we knew people, and even though it was an expensive area, it wouldn't matter because my husband would be a professional like my father: a doctor, a lawyer — someone with an excellent career.

Now don't get me wrong. It isn't that I was looking for a certain type, but coming from the home I came from, those were the types I kept getting set up with. I assumed it was a given: money would never be an issue.

Now what would I do with all of that free time after I married my doctor/lawyer/professional husband? He'd be busy working, so I certainly wouldn't need to work myself. Volunteering! I could become a professional volunteer. I could give art classes to the less privileged. I mean, I wanted to work for personal fulfillment at least until there were too many kids to handle juggling a husband, work, and family.

So in my head I was in Los Angeles with a family, a rich volunteer life, and helping underprivileged children. My husband was tall and handsome and wore a black hat, and I, of course, my new custom sheitel. We were the perfect couple in my mind's eye, and we were going to contribute to the community. Between his work at the hospital/law firm/office and my volunteer work, we were going to make a kiddush Hashem with every step we took.

I was so sure that would be my life that I turned down shidduch opportunities that didn't offer the potential I had come to relish. Then, on a summer vacation in Israel, I went out with the man I was actually going to marry.

He was a professional, all right, only his profession was as a musician working in a wedding band while completing his musical education. It wasn't what I had expected, but I could handle it. Money was never really my goal; the main thing was to help the world. People needed music to dance at weddings. He was doing holy work.

Tall? Well, good thing the person introducing us forgot to mention his height. I forgot to ask. After five minutes

into our first date, height suddenly didn't feel so impor-
tant. He was still five inches taller than I was. We were
actually well suited for each other.

As for Los Angeles, when I realized that my future
husband had every intention of making his home in the
Holy Land, I figured it would be fine. I liked Israel. I
decided that if that's what Hashem wanted, I would
want it, too. Luckily for me the wedding I had pre-
planned in my head took place in Israel outside the city
of Modi'in, on a little moshav commonly referred to as
"The Moshav." I had planned every detail from previous
summer visits to Israel and weddings I'd attended on
the Moshav. The tablecloths would be purple, the flowers
hydrangeas, even the caterer had already been selected
in my mind. All I needed was the right chassan willing
to go along with it.

Well, perhaps Hashem has a sense of humor because
when I shared my dream wedding with my husband-to-
be, he said, "That's funny. I'd never have thought of get-
ting married there. My parents were one of the first fami-
lies to settle on that moshav."

I quickly realized that some of my expectations for
marriage would be realized — like where to have my
dream wedding — and others wouldn't work out, like liv-
ing in Los Angeles, not needing to work, and being able
to be a full-time volunteer.

Something else I realized about marriage is that there
is a reason that in our generation you don't get married
at twelve or thirteen like in generations past. Part of get-
ting married is developing a maturity that allows you to
be flexible when your expectations aren't met, not only in
marriage, but also in life.

Before marriage, I was free to dream and imagine the
life I wanted. Now, in marriage, I realize that everything

I thought I wanted I wouldn't necessarily get. And things that I thought I wanted weren't necessarily for my good, spiritually or otherwise. Although I never imagined I would live in Israel, I thank Hashem every day that this is where He chose for us to build our home. My little boy is bilingual at only two and a half. And when I ask him what he wants to do on our special "yom kef" (fun day) together, he says he wants to go daven at the Kosel.

I'm not a professional volunteer but enjoy volunteering weekly at the local soup kitchen. As for never having to work, I have been blessed, instead, with a fulfilling career where I help people as a therapist and see my work, with Hashem's guidance, making a difference in people's lives.

I'm not saying it's always easy. There are definitely moments I wish I were shopping in Los Angeles or out for Chinese on Pico Boulevard. But if you asked me to trade my life here for the life I thought I wanted, I wouldn't. I have been lucky to receive blessings in my marriage and my life that I couldn't possibly have expected in Los Angeles, or anywhere else for that matter. I thank Hashem for knowing what I needed more than I did and allowing us to live this beautiful life together in His holy city of Jerusalem.

Chapter 2

From Kallah La La Land to Shanah Rishonah

When I was single, I was taught to focus on what *I* wanted out of life. Where did *I* see myself in ten years? What kind of person did *I* want to marry? By the time I was ready to get married, I was more or less aware of the answers to these questions.

I knew how to be me. I was good at that. But after my wedding I learned that being married is more than learning about yourself, about how to have clear goals or aspirations. Early on in marriage, I realized a shift had to be made. To enter this new part of life, I'd have to let go of the idea of me just a little to become part of a "we."

The longer I'm married, the more I realize the dichotomy that lies in the balance of retaining one's individuality and identity and becoming a unit that works together to attain a new identity as a married couple. Working together is important not only for what is good for your husband or yourself, but also for the greater good, for the "we" that we strive to become as a married couple.

Becoming a "we" doesn't happen the moment you step out from under the *chuppah*. Time and effort are necessary when making the shift from me to we, but the outcome, when it is done with integrity and vision, can be beautiful.

It's so easy to get caught up in the excitement of the wedding that you can forget that marriage is both lots of fun and lots of work. The ultimate goal is to remember that you are now involved in something bigger than yourself. You are becoming a partner in creation, not just of your future children but a partner in the "we" you will eventually come to refer to as yourselves. The more aware you are of your own potential for growth and change, the better.

May you be inspired by these stories to create something beautiful when you start to think of yourself and your husband as a unit, the "we" you are engaged in creating.

We Keep on Growing Together
Devorah Leah Romano

When I was engaged, my older sister kept telling me, "You will never really know someone until you live with him." I nodded amicably but internally scoffed at this bit of information. I thought I knew my chassan. After all, we had covered all the important topics on our dates. We had spoken about decision-making, husband and wife roles, the importance of learning together, and whether he would let me drive on long road trips if he was tired. He agreed, but wondered why I asked.

I explained that growing up we took long road trips from Berkeley, California, to Los Angeles to visit my cousins on a pretty regular basis. The same scenario played itself out each time. My father insisted on driving even though he was tired (according to my mother). My mother would then insist he drink coffee, which he would invariably refuse. He claimed he was just fine. My mother would nod off to sleep in the front seat of our fifteen-passenger van and wake with a start every fifteen minutes or so with a cry of "Yud! Are you awake?" Keeping this in mind, I was armed with the aforementioned question.

When you date, they tell you to look for signs of his character: Did he tip the waiter? Did he hold the door open for you? Did he listen attentively when you spoke? They are all good things to keep an eye out for, but a lot of tests of character don't reveal themselves until after you're married.

The third week of our married life, we took a road trip from Berkeley to Los Angeles. After a few days of sightseeing along the way, we finally arrived in Los Angeles, tired and hungry. We ate at a restaurant, and I dropped my husband off at shul to daven while I headed to an appointment I had made weeks earlier. Driving along the main boulevard, I looked to my left and started making a left turn onto a busy street. Boom! A car hit me out of nowhere.

My car spun around and I wasn't sure if I was hurt or not. I took a breath and realized I was still alive. The other car never stopped; it was a hit-and-run. Pulling over to the side of the road, I realized one of the tires had been punctured. I called my mother crying (my husband didn't have a cell phone). She told me to take a deep breath, and, after I had calmed down, she advised me to leave the parked car and walk the half block to my appointment. I'd waited so long and I was only in town for a few days, it wasn't worth missing it. Still shaking, I did so.

While I was sitting in the waiting room, my husband called my cell and I told him what had happened. He reassured me and told me he would meet me outside my appointment when I was ready.

After the meeting, I walked outside and met my husband by the car. He made sure I was situated comfortably, then ran to a grocery store and got me vitamin water. After making sure I was O.K., he changed the tire. Some passerby stopped to help him, and then he got back into the car. The sight of his blackened hands was more beautiful and reassuring to me than any conversation on a date could have been. I had a strong, capable husband who could take care of me.

Before we married, I had gotten used to being single and independent. When we were preparing for our trip, I single-handedly planned the trip, booking hotel rooms and figuring out our itinerary without consulting my husband. When we got there, I was the one who stopped and asked people for directions. Finally my husband commented that he was used to his parents' marriage, where his father would usually ask for directions and his parents would plan trips together.

At first I got defensive and annoyed. But after thinking about it a while, I realized, Wow! I can let go now and have someone take care of me once in a while. I don't have to do all the work. I'm married! It was very liberating to realize this and know I didn't have to do everything alone anymore.

Those first few weeks of marriage were intense! Long conversations learning about each other, our likes and dislikes, our interests and fears, our similarities and differences. We learned teamwork. He would go out and toivel boxes of dishes; I would wash them after he brought them home. We organized the house together, went out to buy furniture together, and prepared meals side by side at the end of a long, tiring day.

Just when I thought we had basically figured out this whole marriage thing, on our three-month anniversary I found out I was expecting. At first, we were thrilled with our little secret. Four weeks later I came home from work feeling nauseous. I told my husband that maybe it was the fish sticks the school I worked in had served for lunch.

When the nausea didn't abate the whole evening, I remembered that along with pregnancy comes morning sickness and realized that this was probably it.

But I had assumed morning sickness was come-and-go mild nausea. My pregnant self discovered that the nausea plagued me twenty-four hours a day, seven days a week. Whether I was lying down, sitting up, and especially at school when we served the kids' lunch, I was nauseated. The worst was Wednesday: fish-sticks-and-rice day. Ginger ale with ice cubes and melba-toast became my new-found diet.

My husband would come home from kollel to find his wife in bed moaning and groaning, a pile of books and crackers on the nightstand. There was no aroma of supper in the air. Where was his happy, charming wife from just a few weeks ago? No marriage book had taught me how to prepare dinner when I had just thrown up or how to greet my husband cheerfully after a long day of constant nausea. All I wanted to do was vent about how I was feeling and spend the evening in bed with a good book reading the night away.

Until now, I was primarily taking care of my husband, making dinner, running the house. Now the roles had changed. My husband prepared toast for me and brought *me glasses of ginger ale and melba-toast snacks late at night and early in the morning. And once, when I came home from work, he had swept the whole apartment and mopped it during his lunch break.*

A lot was changing in our relationship, including the topics of our conversations. Now that we were expecting, our lives revolved around our future baby and our hopes and dreams for him. We had late-night conversations about how we wanted our marriage to be, how we were raised, and how we wanted to raise our kids.

My husband grew up with a Moroccan mother who constantly cleaned and cooked without a complaint. I grew up with a full-time housekeeper and never had to wash dishes or fold laundry. So when I started running my own house, it was a real shocker to realize that those dishes in the sink weren't going to magically get clean by themselves. They would sit there until I decided to wash them!

In my parents' house, we were always thanking and complimenting one another for things others might take for granted. The marriage books all mentioned how important it is to thank and appreciate your spouse for even the smallest thing, like taking out the garbage. So, like a good wife, when my husband took out the garbage, I was overeffusive with my gratitude. "Thanks so much for taking out the garbage! You're amazing! You're such a good husband!" My husband kind of shrugged off the compliments, and I felt kind of hurt.

Meanwhile, when I would wash the dishes or clean up the living room, I was proud of my accomplishments and would wait for my husband to compliment me. Seeing no forthcoming praise, I would go to sleep disappointed.

When we finally discussed this disparity, my husband expressed feeling patronized for being complimented on doing such a minor task such as taking out the garbage. I explained that I was used to being complimented for everything and was saddened when I would do a household chore without any recognition on his part.

Once we realized where the other was coming from, we both made an effort to change. I cut back on complimenting my husband to an extreme and tried to only thank him in an authentic way when what he did really meant a lot to me. For his part, he tried to notice the little things and comment on them. We both felt a lot better after that.

After the baby was born, our lives were turned upside down, preoccupied as I was with changing diapers, learning how to do feedings, taking time to eat, and dealing with a colicky baby. In addition, I was an emotional wreck, crying out of the blue for no apparent reason.

My husband tried to help out as much as he could, but also longed for the days when he could leave the house and go learn without his wife calling him back to change one more diaper. I, on the other hand, was scared to let him go, because I felt like I needed his constant presence for reassurance and help. He felt restricted and tied down and tried to reinstate his independence by leaving the house even more frequently to learn.

We finally went to see a rav, who gave us some very wise advice. "First of all, each of you will never fully understand what the other is going through. You," he said to my husband, "will never know how your wife felt giving birth, recovering from the birth, and dealing with the baby. And you," he said, turning to me, "will never understand your husband's need to go out and learn with his chavrusa."

He said we had to try to be more understanding of each other's needs. He said the day would come when my husband would offer to help me put the kids to bed, and I would tell him, "It's O.K. if you go learn now," and then he'd say, "No, it's O.K., I'm going to stay home and make dinner. . ."

Our first year of marriage was a challenge, and the first year of our baby's life was an adjustment. But we have never stopped growing together. When my husband watched the baby today so I could take a nap and finish writing this, I felt we had arrived.

Who's the Boss?

● Devorah Frank*

When I was a little girl, I hated the idea of being told what to do. My mother loves to tell the story of me at two years old, which she affectionately refers to as the "Who's the boss" story.

The scenario went like this: I would be down on the floor. She would tickle me and ask, "Who's the boss?"

I would giggle and say, "I'm the boss."

Then she would tickle me more and ask again, "Who's the boss?"

"I'm the boss," I would insist.

I was tickled even harder and she would say, "Who's the boss?"

And finally I would give up and say, "You're the boss," and she would let me go.

I would jump up, turn around, look back at her and yell over my shoulder, "But I am the boss of me!"

Those moments in my early childhood pretty much summed me up for most of my life. My independence was such a strong part of me I thought I would never find a suitable marriage partner. It's not that I didn't want to get married, I just wondered if it was possible to find my Mr. Right. Then, as a teen and early in my twenties, especially as friends started to marry, marriage became all I could think about.

Not to say that I didn't do other things. I was productive, very productive. With every year that passed and I wasn't married, I gave myself a new challenge. But everything felt a little less of a simchah without a husband to share it with. I was upbeat and happy but also lonely.

At a certain point, I decided enough was enough; I was going to do what it took to get married. I would move to a new city. Change your makom and change your mazel, the saying goes, so I decided a year in Israel was just what I needed to make it happen.

Six days after landing, I had the zechus of meeting my husband. We knew instantly. The practical girl that I am insisted on us waiting to get engaged. We needed more time — or, at least, I did. It was interesting watching my process although I knew full well this was the man I would marry. I was still too scared and had too many issues to let it happen. I wanted to be my own person. I wanted to continue to be me. How could I do that married?

I am still not entirely sure what happened, maybe it was my fear of commitment, but I told him I wanted to take a break. I wanted to try going out with other people.

"No problem," he said. "You go out with whoever you want. I'll wait."

I am sure it was that instant that told me that we were meant to be together. I never dated anyone else. We were engaged a week later. I realized in retrospect that I just needed to feel that I could still make my own decisions, that I was still an independent thinker.

My husband isn't controlling, baruch Hashem. He doesn't think of himself as the boss of me. And I don't think of myself as his boss either. We have grown to a place of embracing the idea of helpmates. He helps me grow into the person I want to become, and I make it a priority to help him actualize his potential in the world.

When I first came to Israel I couldn't get over the Hebrew word for "my husband," ba'ali. The literal translation is "my master." I had such a dilemma: I had always dreamed of calling someone husband. I wasn't really interested in giving up the dream. On the other hand, the idea of calling someone "my master" was a bit too much for me. Funnily enough, I started to hear the word ba'ali running off my tongue.

The word ba'ali reminds me of another Hebrew term: ba li means "I like it" or "it suits me." When I say "ba'ali," I think about how much he means to me, how lucky I am to have found someone who gets who I am and for whom I can do the same. I think about how much we suit each other. When I call him "ba'ali," I am thanking Hashem for His kindness in giving me a husband who suits me so well.

My husband gets me even though on the surface we are wildly dissimilar. Although I used to look at us and wonder, What are we doing together? We are so different, I realize that on the deepest level each of us is exactly what the other needs. My husband gives me space to be who I need to be. I, in turn, have learned what he needs as well.

I call and ask if he minds if we have Shabbos guests and whom to invite. I know full well he will say yes to whomever I suggest, but he appreciates my taking his feelings into consideration. Before I make plans, I check in with his schedule, making sure my plans work with his instead of just announcing where I am going. Part of being married is respecting each other's need for independence and alone time, as well as respecting the importance of interdependence and togetherness.

Most of all, I have learned that in a marriage there doesn't have to be a "boss." Together we are respecting each other's different needs for autonomy while becoming a new unit where there is no boss, only a partnership of two people working together every day to make the best marriage possible.

Helping My Spouse Shine
━━━━━━━━━━━━━━━━━━━━━━━━━━━━━━━● Marna Becker

After years of being ba'al teshuvah singles and eating countless Shabbos meals out, you would think that the first thing we would do once we were married was open our home to those who needed a meal. To be honest, by the time we actually got to the chuppah, we were both absolutely exhausted as well as delirious with joy that we had each found the "right one."

Together, in our first week of marriage, we made a decision not to have guests during our shanah rishonah, unlike most of the other couples in our community. Many of our friends, especially those who were also newly married, seemed a bit surprised. They were really excited to invite, cook for, and become the "hosts with the most" for their guests. They were enthusiastic, while we were, well, still stunned from our wedding.

After the wedding, we moved into a modest one-bedroom apartment in the Kiryat Moshe neighborhood of Jerusalem. For the first five months of our marriage, I was in Ulpan (intensive Hebrew-language course) part-time while my husband worked full-time. I did most of the cooking for Shabbos on Thursday nights and Friday mornings, and my husband helped out with the shopping. He also assisted me with smaller tasks like chopping vegetables, checking rice, and taking out the garbage. It was a fairly normal arrangement. I enjoyed cooking, which I found relaxing.

After Ulpan ended, I soon found a job working as a client liaison at a financial organization. My work schedule was a bit unusual. My husband worked in the same office park, but his schedule was more traditional. Our lunchtimes never matched up.

While I was not the first person to work on a different schedule than my spouse, it did prove difficult to find time to spend with my husband. I was at work when he was off and vice versa. I also discovered that my husband really preferred me to cook for Shabbos on Friday mornings and not on Thursdays. He thought the food tasted fresher if it was cooked closer to Shabbos. This was very difficult, especially as I had to work until quite late on erev Shabbos. I had to pass the baton to him. And that's how it started.

One day, my husband asked me what ingredients he would need to make sushi. I quickly scribbled a list of ingredients on an empty envelope and gave it to him. I had learned to make sushi in a class as a graduate student, but it had been some years, and I didn't really remember how to roll the sushi properly. But when he asked me if I would show him how to roll sushi, I couldn't refuse his sweet request.

We chose a Friday morning and went to it. The first week I helped, and a couple of weeks later, I came home to find that my husband had rolled the sushi by himself, and his was turning out to be better than mine! Needless to say, I was grinning from ear to ear.

Slowly but surely, my husband started to help prepare other parts of the Shabbos meals. He first held court as the King of Cholent, but later moved on to chicken and kugel recipes when we found that neither of us can successfully digest cholent. He soon developed an interest in other types of food to keep our Shabbos menus from getting boring.

I know what you're thinking. There is nothing remarkable about this story so far. My husband is not the first man since Adam HaRishon to help his wife cook or clean for Shabbos. What makes my husband unusual is that when we got married his entire repertoire was boiling water, making pasta, and assembling burritos. He came from a home where meat was always served "well done" — meaning having the consistency of a hockey puck. Now he's able to make a whole Shabbos in two to three hours if the need arises, though we usually have a bit more time and prefer to work together.

Shanah rishonah is about trial and error. It's about seeing what works and what doesn't. It's about discovering hidden talents and deciding how to best utilize them for the common good of the marriage. It's about building confidence and faith in each other and between each other and bringing out the very best in our spouses.

My husband learned to cook in order to help us as a couple. In the end, he realized he had a talent for and a joy of cooking. He told me that he felt good having such an instrumental role in making Shabbos. My husband filled a niche where he could shine and build his self-confidence as a member of our team. I watched him grow and it was beautiful to witness.

Oh! Those Daily Battles

We have a towel rack made of white plastic. It actually has two racks, each of which is shaped like a stretched-out ches, one rack for him and one for me. Nothing unusual in that, think you. Ah...but this towel rack is very different. This towel rack is my mussar teacher.

I always put his towel neatly on the front rack with his embroidered name facing outward. That's my first test. Hanging up his towel calmly on its rack even when I find it crumpled up and damp on my newly washed floor.

I do hang it back up, don't misunderstand me. I hang it back in its place because of damage control; I really don't like a messy house. Yet, while I am hanging up that damp offering, I can feel my temper rising. If I were a cat, my claws would be out. If I were X-rayed, you would see my knotted stomach. If you took my temper with a "temper-mometer," the mercury would burst out of the glass!

How I do try to place that damp, bedraggled towel lovingly and appreciatively back on its rack! After all, he is my husband. That towel shows me that I have a husband, a someone who is so special in ways I cannot begin to articulate. The kind of specialness that makes me break out in a warm, tender smile should I catch a glimpse of him in a crowd or just hear his voice from the other side of the mechitzah in shul.

Yet how can he be so thoughtless? What does he think I am, his slave? How long does it take just to put his towel away?

Other such raging thoughts burst through my consciousness, obliterating my resolution to be accepting and even feel privileged by the chance to serve my zivug. Each time, I try to catch my temper before it catches me. Wow, it's fast. Nanoseconds.

Now understand, this happens time after time, and I still can't catch myself before the explosion, small though it is. I don't want to get angry. I want to stay calm! Did you see that growl? Even as I merely think about it, my pen sinks its owner's frustration into the paper (that's what exclamation marks are for).

So this week I am going to have a towel-rack campaign. First of all, I am going to take a deep breath and aim for a positively beatific state of mind. Stand up straight: nothing like a good posture to make you feel dignified and in control. No shoulder slouching, please. Head tall, shoulders back, and a calm face with a gentle smile.

Oh! This is just not me. I know that damp towel is waiting for me to hang it up. What's the point of pretending? Let's just go in there, grab it, and get it over with.

"Oh no, you don't, Mr. Yetzer Hara. You won't get me that way. That towel belongs to my hubby, the very man I stood under the chuppah with."

That's what I'll do: I'll pick up the towel and dance it to the towel rack, singing wedding tunes. "La la la, la la, la la la la la... Mee-ee-ee ban siach... Kol sasson v'kol simchah..."

What on earth are you doing?

"I'm dancing my chassan's towel to the chuppah — I mean, towel rack, Mr. Yetzer Hara, that's what I'm doing."

Of course.

"Don't you be patronizing. I have my reasons."

I'm sure you do. What could be more reasonable than dancing with your chassan's towel and singing wedding tunes?

"It stopped me from being angry. What could be more reasonable than that?"

You call it reasonable not to be angry when something has happened that you should be angry about? He carelessly left a damp towel on the floor. Again.

"Don't you try to add more fuel to the fire. I know your ways."

All right, have it your way. Let's see how long you manage to keep this up.

"Oh! Mr. Yetzer Hara, you are really evil."

I try my best! Did I catch a soupçon of temper in your tone? See, that temper of yours is always around the corner. Keep up the good work. See you later.

"Not if I see you first."

Now to put the towel back... Oh, rats! The rack has fallen off again.

You see, the towel rack has a dreadful penchant for falling down. I will be hanging up the freshly laundered towels, and the towel rack will stay apparently well attached to the wall as I hang my husband's towel (that's a lesson in itself: always put husband first). Then I will gingerly start passing my towel over its rack when bloomp — one side of the rack loses its moorings. As I struggle to reattach the rack, the second side comes free, and the towels flip around in a victory dance. Meanwhile, my nostrils flare open trying to breathe out fire, and I growl.

No, that's not how I want to react. I'm just never going to beat my temper. Perhaps I'll just stop trying.

"There you go again, Mr. Yetzer Hara. I will not listen to you. Mr. Towel Rack, shall I put you gently back in your place, or shall I dance with you, too?"

What would your husband say if he caught you dancing with the towel rack?

"He's getting used to my offbeat ways."

And you have to pay for it by putting up with —

"That's enough, Mr. Yetzer Hara. Marriage is all about adjusting."

That must be a quote from a man trying to trick you into simpering obedience.

"Phew, you're laying it on thick. What's the problem? Am I getting too near to being contented with my lot? Am I getting too close to realizing that this test is about my

temper and not about damp towels, loose towel racks, or even my husband?"

Yes, I'm finally getting the right perspective. This towel rack has been such a help. I had thought of buying a new one, but I think I'll wait until I have really overcome my temper. Say, one month without any sort of outburst no matter how many times it falls down.

"There you go again, Mr. Yetzer Hara. Give me impossible targets and then gloat when I fail."

I have a phone call to make.

"Hi, can we buy a new towel rack for our shower?"

"It's a strange time to ask."

"Yes, it really is so vital that I had to phone you in the middle of work. So can I?"

Whatever happened to that independent young lady who made all her own decisions in life?

"Not now, Mr. Yetzer Hara, I'm much too contented to fall for that stuff."

I hang up the phone content, towel rack shopping on my mind. Mr. Yetzer Hara has lost this round.

Unsplitting the Sea

● Juniper Ekman

When I graduated from college, I got my first apartment in Los Angeles: a one-room guesthouse. A sink was my landlord's idea of a kitchen, and a box built into one corner served as a closet. That was it. No cupboards, no dividing walls, no character. Just 160 square feet of scratched white walls and privacy. Well, privacy was what I had wanted, after all.

In this tiny space, I had to fit my life. I had very little furniture: just three bookshelves. I had no cabinets, no counters, nowhere to stash the myriad little things that come from being a pack rat, nor enough shelves for the hundreds of books that come from being an avowed bookworm and the child of two librarians. I needed the trappings of modern life, but I had no budget. Adulthood is expensive, as is life in Los Angeles. Independence and a place of my own had taken up all of the slack in my budget.

Fortunately, Los Angeles is also the land of inexpensive excess. You just have to know where to look.

In the beginning, I just bought everything I liked that fit my needs and my budget. As my tiny space filled up, I became more selective, looking for pieces that filled the strange nooks and crannies that appeared in my apartment, trying to use every inch of space. I looked for furniture with a small footprint to maintain what little spaciousness I could create in a room half the size of your average living room. Fortunately, I'm good at jigsaw puzzles.

I spent hours searching for that perfect something: a shelf only eight inches wide for that tiny, useless space next to the heater where the wall was stained ($15 in Venice Beach). A table that folds out from thirteen inches to thirty-seven inches to sixty-one inches so I could have Shabbos guests ($40 in Pasadena). And, ooh! A farm hutch painted gypsy colors to give me extra counter and cupboard space ($80 in Marina Del Rey). I was convinced that the perfect piece of furniture would transform not only my apartment, but my life.

———

We weren't even married yet when I brought my first find to what would be our new apartment: six matching CD shelves ($30 in the Hollywood Hills).

"They're perfect!" I gushed. "They match your furniture!"

My husband-to-be had a great deal of neutral-colored furniture. Birch veneer shelves, oak veneer bookshelves, even his car was a neutral silver. I objected to it all on the grounds that it was beige. Oak is beige. Birch is beige. Silver, being oh so neutral, is beige.

I loathe beige in its many, unvaried forms. I like color. But I was willing to indulge in my husband-to-be's love of neutrality. At least, in his own office. The rest of the house would be mine.

Back to the shops I went. I found a bed and some shelves. I looked for things that fit our needs and my tastes. Chests of drawers, a fridge, more shelves. I'd tell him about my finds before I made the purchase ("This fits in our bedroom and it's only thirty-five dollars. I can pick it up after work"), but in my mind the deal was already done.

The wedding arrived and my husband continued to be very tolerant of my shopping tendencies. "If you like it, I support you," he frequently said.

But sometimes I bought things because I loved them and they didn't fit the house or our needs. And when you've wasted time and money on something, it's easy to forget that it's just a thing. Things are there to make our lives easier. They're not supposed to be the point of our lives. And still my husband gave (mostly) unwavering support for my purchases. I was frugal, after all. And our house was beginning to feel like a home, even if it was a home overrun by colors. Matching, coordinating, contrasting. It all worked somehow.

Except for the red. I brought home a horizontal, cottage-style paper towel holder in red, a color my husband can't stand. It took up a foot of counter space in our tiny kitchen and unrolled too easily.

"Do we really need that?" my husband asked.

"I need it," I replied. "It has a drawer!"

"Do you need it more than we need our counter?"

"Aesthetically," I insisted. "It matches my dishes!"

Not a good argument. My husband hates my dishes. I collected them over many years, long before we met and married. Red with white stripes, white with red polka dots, all different lovely reds.

"I find it jarring."

"I find it charming."

But here's the thing: we weren't a couple of "I's" anymore. We were an "us" now, a "we." It took consciously remembering that to avoid stepping on each other's toes or leaving each other out in the cold. This process of "unsplitting the sea," of two people becoming one unit and making a comfortable, uplifting home together, was going to take time. In the meantime, this home had to work for the both of us. And in the end, it was just stuff.

So my lovely red cottage-style paper towel is still in the house. It sits on top of the refrigerator, in the back, awaiting a time when I can let go of my attachment to it and allow it to find a new home or our first yard sale, whichever comes first. Red is off the list now. No matter how much I like it, whatever it is, unless I'm willing to paint it, I let it go. My husband is right; it is a little jarring, even if it's nicely coordinated. And I'm giving away most of my old red dishes, the ones I once thought would grace my holiday tables. Instead we're choosing new dishes, new themes, something we both love (we're still looking). He loves my other color choices, or at least quietly tolerates them.

In the meantime, he found an upright paper towel holder at Target.

"Chrome O.K.?" he asked.

We bought the antique copper one. It does what it's supposed to do and only takes up about six inches. It'll grow on me. Eventually.

Let's Talk About It!: Communication Is the Key

Recently, I was trying to contact a writing student of mine. I called once. No answer. I waited for a reply. Hours passed, still no answer. I called again and the call went straight to voice mail. An hour later I tried again, and again the call went straight to voice mail. I called another student to make sure I had the correct number. She verified it and suggested that I call the student's husband and see if he could help me locate her.

After three rings he picked up.

"Hello, this is Shifrah Devorah Witt, your wife's writing teacher. Do you know how I can find her?"

He replied that she was right beside him and handed her the phone.

"The funniest thing happened," she explained. "I couldn't find my phone all day. Tonight when I was doing the dishes and I got to the end of the pile, at the bottom of my sink there it was. Sopping wet, as you can imagine. It doesn't work anymore."

I realized what a profound lesson it was. Sometimes in life we try to communicate; we try to get through. But we keep going straight to voice mail. It's as though we are reaching out, but the person we are trying to call just isn't picking up the phone. Or, worse, we have a shaky connection and can't really hear what it is we are being told. As frustrating as this can be over the phone, in real life when this happens, especially when it happens with someone you love, it can be even more frustrating.

A huge part of marriage is the ability to hear your spouse, communicate your own needs and wants in a way that he can hear you, and find a language that you share as a couple in which you can communicate effectively with one another. It's not enough to know that you are dialing the right number: you have to make sure the line isn't waterlogged and thus going straight to voice mail.

Shortly after my husband and I got married, we realized that even though we were both native English-speakers (though he is also fluent in Hebrew), we frequently found ourselves in the midst of miscommunications, what we liked to call language barriers. He grew up in Jerusalem and I grew up in California. I was hearing his words, but often things were getting lost in the translation, whether it was the way he spoke or the way I understood or vice versa.

The classic examples of these types of funny communication blips include the time I asked him if he could go grocery shopping. He said, "Don't worry. I'm on top of the ball." It took a minute to realize he was attempting the American expression "on the ball," and translating it into Hebrew in his head and then back to English.

Another time I suggested a sugar-free diet for both of us, and he kindly looked at me and said, "No problem. I'll quit, cold meat." That one took a minute to translate: he meant "cold turkey." I couldn't stop laughing.

Though these funny moments soften the harder moments of communication barriers, I eventually learned that just as we came from different households, we had different styles of communicating.

I came from a home where things were said directly without any extra niceties. In our home, if the garbage needed to be taken out, the request was stated clearly: "Please take out the garbage." My husband grew up in a completely different manner. His mother never demanded. She would gently ask, "Does someone want to do a mitzvah and take out the garbage for Ima?"

Though neither way is right or wrong, it did cause a certain amount of confusion at first. I didn't realize what was so terrible about my asking him directly to take out the garbage, and he didn't understand why I wasn't asking in a sweeter, gentler way. To me it was such a simple request; it didn't need those extra syllables. To him, he wasn't being treated kindly or respectfully, which, of course, wasn't my intention.

Each couple will have communication issues to work on. The important thing is to identify your communication issues and style when they come up and work on them. Letting things fester is never a good solution, nor is hoping things will blow over. It's important to learn how to communicate effectively with each other from the get-go. *B'ezras Hashem*, you're going to be together for a very long time, and the faster you establish a language that works for you as a couple, the happier and healthier you can become.

Remember, this is the person you are going to be talking to for a very long time. You want to make sure the line you're dialing isn't sitting at the bottom of a sink full of dishes, waterlogged and unavailable to take your call.

The Key to Communication

● *Chana Herzog*

"*Trust me. The key to a successful marriage is communication.*" *How many times have you heard that one? From the moment we got engaged, our conversations with parents, aunts, uncles, older siblings, and married friends always ended up with them telling us how to have a healthy marriage. I would nod, smile, and say, "Thanks for that... Mmm-hmm, I'm sure..."*

Communication! How obvious is that? I wasn't so naïve that I did not realize that every couple has their challenges, and I'd heard the line "Marriage is work." But we were blissfully happy, and my chassan could do no wrong in my eyes. We knew exactly what we were doing.

A lot of times, when I observed couples, I would make mental notes. Oh no, don't do that, I would think as I observed the wife who constantly complained, "I can't cope! Where were you? I'm so tired!" Poor guy. She's really annoying. Don't be annoying, I told myself.

Then there was the high-maintenance wife. Her husband was working as hard as he could, and he was stressed trying to keep up with her demands. She constantly needed manicures and pedicures, designer clothes and diamonds. Her husband felt inadequate if he couldn't keep up with her demands, and she had no regard for his hard work. Don't be like her, I noted.

My all-time favorite wife to observe was the one who let her husband be himself. She wasn't needy; she was confident and had things under control. She always seemed to be in a good mood. She wasn't on a mission to change him because she accepted him for who he was. She was his best friend. Be like her. She's a good wife.

We must have been married for about two months when I learned what it really means to communicate. It was Chanukah time and we had just moved to Israel. We were thrilled to be living in the Holy Land and couldn't wait to settle down and start our lives. There were a lot of get-togethers going on for the young kollel crowd, and we were finding it a bit hard to keep up with it all. We were just settling in and were still in our own world of bliss, not feeling the need to spend our evenings with anyone else.

It was the third night of Chanukah, and we were invited to a drop-in Chanukah party. Honestly, I wasn't desperate to go, but a lot of my friends that I hadn't seen for a while would be there, and I felt that we shouldn't completely isolate ourselves socially. My husband had expressed his complete lack of interest in attending, triggered by the fact that a few of his friends were getting together to play basketball that night. He'd rather play in the game.

Should I tell him that I want us to drop by the Chanukah party? Should I force him to do something he doesn't want to do? I remembered that wife I had observed, that wife who was her husband's best friend. That wife who wasn't controlling and just let her husband be. I remembered how much I wanted to be like her.

I prepared myself in my head. Chana, this isn't about you. He wants to play in the game. You have to be selfless. So I didn't tell my husband that I wanted us to pop into the party. I told him he could go to his game. He was ecstatic. He told me he had the coolest wife a guy could ever dream of.

Lucky you, I thought. So I pretended it didn't bother me that we weren't going to the party. But I kept think-

ing about the party and that maybe we should have gone. Everyone would think we were snobby and didn't want to have anything to do with them. And who cared about a basketball game? Whether his team won or lost wouldn't make a major difference in any of our lives.

My husband called me at half-time. "Chana, are you sure you wouldn't rather go to the party?"

"I'm sure. Just continue your game."

I was being a martyr. I would sacrifice what I wanted for the sake of our marriage.

His team won the game. My husband came home that night feeling good. The next morning, my friend called me.

"Why didn't you guys come to the party? It was so nice! We missed you!"

I rattled off an excuse and hung up the phone, angry. I turned to my husband, and our conversation went something like this:

"Why didn't we go to the party? We should have gone! Is your obsession with basketball going to rule our lives?"

He looked at me blankly. "I thought you didn't even want to go."

"I did want to go!"

"So why didn't you say so?"

"Because I knew that you wanted to play in that basketball game."

"If I would have known you really wanted to go, I would have gone."

"So I should have said I wanted to go?"

"Of course you should have!"

"But then you wouldn't be happy. You'd be thinking about how you wish you could have played in that game, and I forced you to go..."

"I'd rather you be happy than me play basketball!" he exclaimed.

"So you could have gone to play the basketball game, and we could have dropped by afterward," I suggested.

"That would have worked. Then we'd both be happy."

And that was when the lesson was learned. I was trying so hard to be the perfect wife that I had stopped communicating. I needed him to know what I really wanted without having to say it. And if he didn't get it, then I would be selfless and put my needs aside. But little did I know that by neglecting to communicate what I was really feeling, I would end up blaming him. I would end up tallying up brownie points of all the times I was selfless and then hold it against him. I would be the altruistic wife who never really got what she wanted. That's when I understood what they were all saying about communication.

Being my husband's best friend didn't mean that I had to disregard my own needs. It meant that I could tell him anything, and then we could figure it out together.

Don't You Love Me?: A Story About My Husband, Myself, and the Garbage

● Debbie Lublin*

"If you loved me, you would know what I need," I sobbed.

My husband looked at me, bewildered. "You know I love you. If you would just tell me what could make this right, I would do it happily."

"I shouldn't have to tell you," I gasped, glancing in the direction of the garbage.

My husband was dumbfounded. "I'll do anything. Just tell me what it is you want."

"The garbage. I want you to empty the garbage without being asked."

"Is that all? Why didn't you just tell me?"

Yup, that pretty much sums up my first year when it comes to housekeeping. Not the entire year, but a lot of it. What seemed obvious to me was confusing to him. What seemed confusing to me seemed obvious to him. What took a long time to figure out was that we came from totally, I mean totally, different backgrounds. Yes, technically they were similar, but we were raised as different as two people from the same culture could have been.

You see, for me having him take out the garbage without my asking meant he was anticipating my needs and showing that he cared. For my husband, it was simply something he had never done growing up. His mother had a different philosophy from mine: she was raising Torah scholars, and es pas nisht, in her mind, for them to be taking out the garbage. So when my husband walked by a full garbage can, he wasn't engaging in a silent protest; he was just doing what had been expected of him his whole life, focusing on more important things.

For me, raised in a more egalitarian household, I was in pain every time he walked past the garbage. It took me far too long to realize that what I was experiencing as a declaration of my husband's love or lack of love was simply a cultural difference for him. What took me even longer to realize was that if I was clear about my needs and wants for help around the house, I had a better chance of having my needs met than if I sulked, cried, or gave him the silent treatment.

One thing you have to keep in mind as a newly married is that men are literal. If something isn't spelled out for them, it may not occur to them. I now realize that if I want the garbage emptied, I have to ask or leave it in a spot that we have predetermined as a sign the garbage needs to go out. Baruch Hashem, my husband is very happy to help as long as he knows what help I need. One of the biggest challenges for me has been to learn how to communicate clearly and realize that my husband's taking out the garbage or not has absolutely nothing to do with how much he loves me, but how well I communicate my needs.

I suggest that every couple figure out as early on as possible what they need to feel loved, what help they need around the house, and whose job is whose. It can save you time and energy and lots of unnecessary hurt feelings.

"Ostrich" and Other Lessons in Communication

— Rochel Boyde

Not all good people are blessed with good communication skills. For many of us, communication is a learned behavior that we must make a conscious effort to develop. Prior to marriage, my husband and I were both confident in our individual communication skills. My friends always came to me for advice and guidance. His friends always looked to him for understanding and acceptance. So naturally, we assumed that together we would never have an issue. We were wrong.

It took us a while to learn how to talk so the other would hear. It took us even longer to learn how to listen to what the other was not saying.

My husband and I were raised in very different types of homes. Sure, we both came from loving and supportive environments. However, our families could not be more different. My husband's family is polite, respectful, and sensitive to each other. My husband thrives on the pervasive calm that filled his house growing up. My family, on the other hand, consists of people who rarely use "indoor voices," are brutally honest with each other, and can *give a good ribbing, as well as take it. I love the constant chatter and fits of laughter that permeated my childhood home.*

Neither way is right or wrong. Yet, because we are both very much products of the households in which we were raised, we quickly learned that we needed to create an atmosphere in our home that was uniquely our own.

Needless to say, once we were married, it took time to establish an environment that was unique to our individual personalities and yet respectful of our differences. At first, I thought that the onus was on my husband to get used to my sense of humor and not take things so personally. After all, I knew that I never meant anything bad by what I said. Over time, I grew to understand that the responsibility was mine to treat him in a way that he found respectful, just as it was his responsibility to interact with me the way I wanted and needed.

I'm not saying that I changed my personality. But I worked hard to refine my sense of humor, to have more patience when speaking to him, and to notice when his body language tells me that something is wrong.

Similarly, I did not want my husband to change. I married him because I saw amazing qualities in him that convinced me that he would make a terrific husband and father. What I wanted was for my husband to understand that sometimes I crave a little extra attention, sometimes I want him to listen to my concerns no matter how minor they might be, and sometimes I simply want to be able to sit in silence knowing that things are good.

Neither of us was trying to change the other; we were simply trying to learn how to live together. We needed to learn how to communicate—how to be patient with the other's unique manner of speaking and listening. My husband has learned that silence is not a bad thing and that some-

times it's O.K. to think through an issue (read: argument) before hashing it out and resolving it. I've learned that if I don't smile at my husband when he walks in the door, he assumes that something might be wrong. So now, even if I'm busy and absorbed in my work, I make a point of greeting him at the door with a big smile and asking him how his day went.

It's obvious that men and women communicate differently. There are dozens of popular books to that effect. Yet it can be very hard to put that knowledge into practice when we are absorbed in daily life. Every time my husband leaves the house, I tell him to be careful. He views this as a statement that I believe him to be a child who must be protected and warned against imaginary danger. I view it as a way that I tell him I care about him and that I care what happens to him.

I have an incredibly dry sense of humor; there is no joke I can't deliver with a straight face. It took a long time for my husband to learn how to read me. He was never sure when I was being serious and when I was just giving him a hard time. Finally, after more misunderstandings than I care to recall, we decided we needed a "safe word" — a word that either of us could use at any time to indicate that we were in an uncomfortable situation and would function as a quick and easy way to let the other know that it was time to be serious. We chose "ostrich" for the touch of frivolity it added to an otherwise humorless situation.

Though "ostrich" began as a short-term solution that we used multiple times per day, we still find ourselves using it multiple times per week. Sure, we've gotten really weird stares from strangers who overhear us having a con-

versation about ostriches, but I'm more concerned about keeping my marriage conflict-free than I am about disapproving outsiders. Having the ability to step outside of any discussion, debate, joke, or argument with a safe word has made our transition to married life much simpler.

I know the whole "ostrich" thing sounds silly, but it has been a lifesaver. It has prevented many hurt feelings that would have otherwise been caused by ill-timed jokes. "Ostrich" allows me to be myself, and it reassures him that my intentions are good and our marriage is stable.

Once we overcame the first few hurdles, we realized that our conversations often revolved around the mundane trivialities — like chores, errands, and schedules. In an effort to develop a deeper relationship, we instituted a once-a-week date night. It gets us out of our apartment. It encourages us to try new things and explore more. But most importantly, it gives us a chance to reconnect away from computers, cell phones, and our never-ending to-do lists. Whether a fancy restaurant dinner or a casual stroll around town, the point is for us to talk and ensure our bond is not only established and secure but also growing.

Just tonight, my husband walked in the door with a dozen long-stemmed roses, a bag of fresh peaches, and a promise to make dinner so I could relax. I didn't ask for the help. Nor did I tell him how busy my daily routine has gotten. But he knew anyway, because we've worked hard to ensure that we can anticipate the other's needs and react accordingly. At the end of the day, it doesn't matter that there are still dishes in the sink; it matters that our marriage is strong thanks to our efforts.

Don't get me wrong. We aren't the perfect couple that never argues. My husband and I have very different *ways of looking at the world. We have different priorities and often do not understand the other's point of view. Recently, we had a heated discussion about the concept of trust.*

To him, trust covers everything past, present, and future. It means that there are no doubts or concerns no matter what and we know, inherently, that will never change. To me, even though I trust my husband and my marriage fully, I still want to be actively strengthening our bond and working hard to make sure that even far into the future there will never be any reason for us to worry about what the other is doing.

One example is our shared finances. Though my husband and I share a bank account, the one I had while I was single is still open, mostly because I've been too lazy to close it. My husband trusts that I'm not hiding money, and he is O.K. with me having my own bank account. I, on the other hand, don't like the idea of having my own bank account because I want it to be obvious to him that I don't hide shopping sprees or other expenses.

Mind you, the trust isn't the issue. The issue is that we have different styles of communicating that trust. I communicate trust by putting everything out in the open. My husband communicates trust by allowing me to have space.

Often we find that even when our end goal is the same, we present ourselves very differently. I cannot tell you how many times we've found ourselves arguing only to realize afterward that we were both saying the same thing. When I learned how to listen to my husband, and vice versa, our marriage flourished. It's not enough to listen to what your spouse is saying. You must also consider what isn't being said, what's been said previously, and the point of the whole conversation. Keeping in mind that my husband and I have the same values often reminds me that our outlooks aren't as different as I once thought.

Marriage isn't necessarily easy, but it is extremely fulfilling. Working together to forge a bond is always satisfying. Clichés exist for a reason: communication is key to a healthy relationship. My husband and I have so much fun together. We're constantly laughing and enjoying life. We've worked hard to get to this point, and it is so worth it.

Acceptance

●—————————————————————————————————— *Pessy Cohen**

I was so frustrated. Really angry. Relax, I told myself. It's only a box. For sure by Shabbos it will be put away. But it wasn't. And so I had the whole Shabbos to glare at the box sitting next to my front door without saying a word.

It's only a box. It's not a big deal.

The problem was that it wasn't only a box. It was a box that I needed put away. A broken bed that I needed fixed, a sukkah that was waiting to be dismantled, a place to stay that had to be arranged, and myriad other things that I needed taken care of. Why does it take him forever to get things done? I was so annoyed. But I was also so frustrated — at myself.

I was working very hard at trying to give up control to my husband: by letting him do things his way, by reminding myself to accept that this was the way he was. But I was still resentful. Why wasn't this working? Time and time again I said to myself, This time you will not nag. You will not remind, you will not even hint. Just let him take care of it on his own. But here I was back to square one, struggling so hard with myself. And the box is still sitting there, I thought bitterly.

What would happen if I could really let go? I asked myself. If I truly let him take the responsibility for the things that he needs to do? That was when I realized something very important: under the anger was a lot of fear. I was afraid of missing out on things in life. I was afraid of not getting what I needed, of not being taken care of.

O.K., but where do I go from here? I asked myself. I was starting to get nervous again. We were meant to be traveling home to Australia for Pesach and my husband hadn't yet looked into tickets. It was getting closer, and I felt the familiar tension as I moved to remind (read: nudge) my husband to get moving on them.

Just one minute, I told myself. Listen to what your fear is telling you. Instead of pushing away my emotions, telling them to go away, or pretending they didn't exist, I made room for them and allowed myself to hear what they were saying.

In place of my usual tactics of control, I used words to communicate. I communicated my fear:

"I get really nervous when things aren't taken care of and I don't know what's happening," I told my husband. "Would you call the travel agent just for my peace of mind?"

"O.K., no problem," he said. "Could you remind me tomorrow?"

Sure enough, the next day he called the travel agent and booked the tickets. I was amazed. I'd spent all this time in the past trying not to get angry. Again and again I'd just end up even angrier. When I communicated what I needed, my husband was there for me and got the tickets.

I am now learning how to work with my emotions instead of suppressing them. I am focusing on communicating my needs and looking at each experience as another opportunity to get to know myself and my communication

style better. It's a process, a journey, and I never imag-
ined that just one step would already effect changes in
my reality.

Shanah Rishonah, the Second Time Around
Ruth Himmelman

It was the early spring of 1998. I was dreaming about my
late husband. He slowly placed his clothes into his suit-
case when I heard him say, "It's time to say good-bye."

I awoke the next morning in a cold sweat, both
relieved and fearful of what to make of my dream. A
whole year had gone by since my husband, Zelig, had
passed away from leukemia. I was a twenty-eight-year-
old widow with an eighteen-month-old baby boy won-
dering when I would be ready to move on and remarry.
Even more important in my mind was the question of
how. How could I possibly move on? As sad as I felt, I
took my dream as a sign: the time had come. It was time
for the next stage in my life.

I tearfully packed all the sentimental pictures of Zelig
in a box. I called Elisheva, my favorite shadchan, and
nervously gave her the green light to start looking for me.
It was not easy, but I knew I had to move on for the sake
of my little boy, Ezri. He needed a father even more than
I needed a husband.

I will never forget the first time I went out on a date
after my husband's passing. I felt like a young seminary
student going out with a boy for the first time. Like a girl
going on her first date, I attacked my wardrobe with grit-
ted teeth and threw all my clothes onto my bed, trying to
decide what I should wear. Only now, I also had to decide
what head covering to wear! Should I wear a sheitel? Or
a hat? Or maybe a scarf?

I was nervous and anxious. What would I talk about? On the date I made the inevitable mistake. I spoke about my deceased husband. I remember the first thing I did when I came home. I raced to my freezer. I frantically grabbed the Ben & Jerry's vanilla ice cream, tore the lid open, and, having eaten my share of comfort food, cried myself to sleep. Hashem, I prayed, please let this stage in my life not take too long. There is only so much I can take. I don't want to be alone anymore. Please have rachmanus on me.

And then it happened.

In the middle of June, I met Tzvi. It was beautiful to see how he interacted with Ezri. He was caring, devoted, and charming. Their affection for each other appeared to be genuine and real. I knew he was wonderful with my son, but the question remained, was he right for me?

Before long, we were engaged and married. The week of sheva berachos was total bliss. We became the royal family reigning over the sacred land of Har Nof. Everywhere we went we were hosted with lavish Shabbos and yom tov invitations. We were not the average chassan and kallah. We were special because Tzvi was the bachelor who had married a widow with a young son. We walked on cloud nine and had smiles glued to our faces. We were finally happy.

At last we settled into our family routine. Ezri started preschool and Tzvi returned to yeshivah. Our lives began to slowly mesh. It took me time to get used to a few things I normally wouldn't think of. Once I accepted a guest to come for a Shabbos meal, and I casually mentioned it to my new husband. He looked at me kind of strangely. Why are you looking at me like that? I wondered. He finally told me he preferred to have me discuss it with him first before making any decisions. "I'd like it if we make decisions together," he told me gently.

My face dropped. What do you mean? I have to discuss every little thing with you before making any decisions? I thought. Is this normal? I didn't have this with Zelig. It was a new concept for me. But being the wife I wanted to be, I wanted to please Tzvi. I wanted to make him happy, so in the future I tried to discuss questions like this with him before answering them.

In the beginning of our marriage, I did the laundry and the grocery shopping like any other housewife. The clothes weren't done as efficiently as he had done them when he was single, but as long as the clothes were clean, dried, and put away, I was fine with it. I soon learned my husband had his ways of doing things and that laundry was one of them.

One day it dawned on me like a bolt of lightning. An "aha" moment if ever there was one, and I finally understood. He simply enjoyed running the washing machine. Not only that, but he didn't like the laundry getting piled up. At first, I was very bothered by this. I felt like he was stepping over the line. This was my job! However, in time, I soon discovered he was more efficient than I was at laundry, and I didn't mind it anymore.

I wanted to make our home a number-one priority. I wanted my home to be a bayis ne'eman b'Yisrael, and I didn't want any conflicts. But we had different styles. Tzvi liked our home tidy and neat. But I still asked myself, What's the harm if it isn't? Zelig didn't mind if it was a bit unkempt. Thanks to what I learned in my shalom bayis class, I soon understood the value of what my home should look like: what was important to my husband should be important to me.

Communication was another issue. It was a form of art. Getting my point across didn't come easily to me. I had to take a crash course in how to talk to my husband so that he could listen and how to listen so that he could talk and remain blissfully married. I didn't grow up with a strong sense of my own voice like my husband did. I was quiet and introverted, while Tzvi was outgoing and fun. Yet we still managed to get along.

It took time and a great deal of effort to learn and grow through each other's mistakes. I quickly learned the hard way. Instead of brooding over spilled milk, I learned to express myself better. Instead of crying over something he said, I learned to not take things personally. I learned to take deep breaths before I spoke. I learned that the first year of marriage, whether it's the first time around or the second, can have lots of difficult adjustments.

When I first married Tzvi, I was given a piece of advice. Shanah rishonah is not the first year of getting to know each other, but the first five years. When we had at last reached our fifth anniversary, I finally understood what that meant. It means it takes a lifetime to get to know each other, not just the first year.

Hashem has been very good to me. With all the suffering I went through, I never thought I would see the light at the end of the tunnel. All I saw was darkness and loneliness. I saw tears and the fear of being left alone to raise my son. I was disconnected from the world around me and especially from Hashem. I felt abandoned and broken.

Since I've remarried, the black void has been lifted and the rays of sunshine have taken its place. I see my nisayon as a blessing in disguise. It gave me life experience and an opportunity to grow into someone who can overcome anything. I learned that if I could have the courage to watch my husband die before me and raise my son on my own, I could handle anything. It gave me the backbone to withstand any test of emunah and bitachon and solely rely on Hashem and His infinite wonders when life's issues occur.

Most of all, my relationship with Him has grown and blossomed in the most wonderful way. I truly believe He is my Father in Heaven. He was with me when Zelig passed, when it seemed like He was nowhere to be seen. He continues to be with me now and shower me with love, simchah, and an abundance of blessings. I give thanks every day for giving me a chance to remarry. I am so grateful that Hashem gave me Tzvi and the chance to raise my family, happily married and with complete joy.

If You Can't Hear Yourself, How Can You Hear Your Husband?

● Devorah Frank*

My mother is a marriage and family therapist. My grandmother is also a therapist, who focuses on communication. And me, well, maybe it's genetic; people just like to talk to me. I have become the person people go to when they need a little help making sense of their lives.

I'm good at giving advice; I always have been. I like helping people, and I like to talk. I used to get into trouble for it in the second, third, and fourth grades. It wasn't really until college when class discussions were encouraged and valued that I stopped getting into trouble for my love of language and decided to turn it into a career. Today I am a writer, and I offer therapeutic writing techniques to my students to help them find their voice and their words.

So you can imagine how difficult it was when I got married and couldn't find my own words. After so much devotion to others' ability to communicate clearly and effectively, I was shocked to find that I had plenty to work on with my own communication style when it came to talking to my husband.

It must have started during sheva berachos: my husband loves parties and allowed us to accept, not one sheva berachos invitation a night, but also lunch sheva berachos (he's very popular) for each day. There were so many people we wanted to celebrate with. I didn't know how to tell him that the idea of double sheva berachos sounded exhausting and I was still tired from the whirlwind of wedding preparations. If I had told him, he would have done things differently in a second — he's that kind of person — but I didn't. I knew it mattered to him, so I got dressed up twice a day and tried to enjoy myself.

The week we moved into our apartment, one month after our wedding, I insisted on making Shabbos. We didn't have a stove or heat yet, but I was aching to return the kindness so many had showed me over the years. I insisted on having fifteen guests with only a Crock-Pot and a hot plate to cook with. When he offered to help, I said, "No, you go learn. I can handle it."

I came to the Shabbos table exhausted and frustrated. I couldn't enjoy anything because I was still mad about having all the work on my shoulders even though he had offered to help. I had refused his help, devoted to the idea of what I thought a good wife was.

Then things got even more interesting. We loved hosting for Shabbos and were happy to invite as many people as we could fit in our tiny apartment. Well, I guess the word got out that we were open for business. I started getting calls at 3:30 on Friday.

"Can we come for Shabbos?" a voice on the other end of the phone would ask.

"Who exactly?" I would ask.

"Oh, just me and two of my roommates from yeshivah."

It was a mitzvah to have guests, so I would add dish after dish to the menu to accommodate our late guests with Shabbos a few hours away. I hated being called so late, but I didn't know it was all right to say, "Sorry, we're full this week. Next week, please call earlier." It didn't seem like the mentschlich thing to do. So I remained quiet and then watched as our guests ate both our Friday-night dinner and our Shabbos lunch by eleven o'clock at night.

I was getting more and more frustrated. If I was being gracious and hospitable and doing the mitzvos of being a good wife and hosting guests, why did I feel so angry?

Finally I spoke to a friend about my feelings of frustration and being taken advantage of.

"I am so mad, I don't know what to do with myself."

She looked at me and asked a question that changed my life. "Who are you mad at? Your husband and your guests? Or yourself? They ask, you answer. No one is making you agree to things that don't really work for you."

I can't say my behavior changed overnight. It took work to be able to make a connection between what I was thinking and feeling and the words coming out of my mouth. In all honesty, I'm still working on it. But I did start the process, and it is one I continue to this day.

Now, when people call on Friday or even if it is a Wednesday, and it just isn't a good week for us, I have learned to say, "We would love to have you another time. This week just won't work out." I have also learned to accept help from my husband when he offers it instead of feeling that the perfect wife is one who is responsible for every aspect of the house and the marriage. Now, when my husband asks a question like, "Do you want to go away for Shabbos?" I don't feel like I have to always say *yes to accommodate him. I have learned to check in with what I really want in addition to taking his needs into account.*

Recently I had the opportunity to practice being real with my husband and myself. For us, every motza'ei Shabbos is date night. Last week, I was so tired I wanted to cry by the time Havdalah rolled around. In retrospect, I realize I was at the beginning of a cold. At the time I thought I was just tired. It wasn't anyone's fault. I'd taken a nap; I just didn't feel good. I started to think about our evening out, how important it was to my husband, and I didn't want to disappoint him.

Then I took a look at myself. I was finished: there was nothing left of me. So I said, "Honestly, I'm not feeling that great. Would you mind if we stayed home? We could spend time together here and still have our date. We just won't leave the house to have it."

A huge smile of relief washed over his face. "I'd love that. I'm really tired, too. Great idea."

It was interesting for me to watch our interaction and feel like we were traveling on the road of healthy communication. I felt free enough to express what was real for me, and he could not only hear it, but was in total agreement. It made me feel good to think of how far we had come and happy to know we were growing in the area of communication.

I wish I had been able to master this skill of listening to myself and becoming a healthier, happier wife in the very beginning of my marriage. But I am in the continual process of learning. My wish for every Jewish marriage is to realize how important communication is both in the ability to hear yourself and your spouse and to find your own clear language in which to communicate.

Communicating in Marriage

●────────────────────────────── Rachel Rose, M.Sc.

Many newlyweds come out of their courtship full of expectations that everything they have ever dreamed of in marriage will simply "come their way." Especially for those who come from difficult homes, it's easy to imagine their new spouse will be able to make up for all the pain and the love they didn't get in their childhood. That can happen if you're lucky, but more often than not, it takes a lot of work.

In my practice, I have found that the single most productive investment in building a new marriage is developing a healthy communication style, right from the beginning. Here are my top ten communication-building tools, with practical examples of communication that needs some work, and communication that is effective and positive:

1. *Listen. One of the most valuable and sometimes underutilized forms of communication is listening. When you actively listen to your spouse, you send the message that you care. Stop whatever you are doing, make eye contact, and listen with an open mind and heart when your spouse wants to speak to you. The goal of effective listening is to be able to understand and connect with your spouse. Do your best to listen until the end, without interrupting.*

    Avoid listening in order to refute what your spouse is saying. Be empathetic. Empathy is the ability to empathize with your spouse. It isn't feeling bad for the other person, but it is realizing and validating that whatever the other is going through is difficult and he or she has a right to his or her feelings. Try to communicate interest in hearing more about what the speaker has to say. Just being there with your spouse can mean a lot.

Communication style that can use some work:

"Oh, yeah! When that happens to me, I always. . ." (This kind of response brings the conversation back to the listener and can feel invalidating to the speaker.)

Positive communication:

"Really? And then what did you do?" (This response communicates your interest in what the speaker has to say.)

2. *Accept and celebrate differences. When we date, we are often attracted to each other's differences. When we marry, it is often just those differences that drive us crazy. The feeling that our way is the only right way to do things can take the very differences we once found delightful and turn them into what feels like our worst enemy. From a black-and-white perspective, if one person is right, then the other one has to be wrong.*

Develop the gray. You can validate each other's opinions and still agree to disagree. When both spouses work on accepting that there is more than one "right" answer, you create more room in your relationship.

Return to the appreciation that you had for the differences when you were dating. Appreciate and flow with differences rather than allowing them to become a source of conflict. Let go of having to be right.

Communication style that can use some work:

"We always ate gefilte fish for the first course in my house growing up; that's the right thing to eat on Shabbos."

Positive communication:

"I like gefilte fish for the first course; you like salmon. I'll just make a smaller portion of each one, so that we both have what gives us oneg Shabbos."

3. *Validate. When a woman talks about a difficulty she is experiencing, she may be looking for a solution, but more likely she is looking for validation. On the other hand, if she's not sure what type of help she needs, she should try to take a minute to decipher what she needs at that moment. Does she need a solution to a problem or does she simply need to be heard? Sometimes feeling heard and understood can be even more gratifying than finding a solution, and sometimes the problem that needs solving is just that, the need to be heard.*

   Even if you don't agree with what your spouse chose to do in a certain situation, you can validate what he is feeling. Helping your spouse to name the emotion that he is feeling is validating.

Communication style that can use some work:

   "How could you lose your temper like that? Sometimes you act like such a baby!"

Positive communication:

   "Wow! That must have been so frustrating, to wait on line at the bank and have the teller pick up a personal call just when it was your turn!"

4. *Be willing to share. This creates flow in a marriage. Some people believe that small talk is just that: small. Yet it is the consistent sharing of the little events in each other's lives that are the threads that create the fabric of a connected life. It also helps each spouse to be understanding when they know what the other is going through.*

Communication style that can use some work:

   "What do you mean, how was my day? I just barely lived through it and you want me to go through it again?"

Positive communication:

"I really had a tough day. I got stuck in bad traffic on the way to work, and I was late to a very important meeting. My boss heard about it and threatened to fire me if I don't shape up."

5. *Stay positive. You can focus on what there is, or you can focus on what is missing. We always seem to find what we are looking for, so look for the good. Think about it: would you want to do anything for a person who spoke to you in a condescending, critical way? How do your words sound after they have left your lips? Are they soft and gentle or harsh and critical? Are they words of appreciation or words of rebuke? Appreciation builds a relationship, and relationship is what motivates the desire to do things to please your spouse. Often the more you can express appreciation, the more you can hope to receive from your spouse.*

   Make generous deposits into your marital-satisfaction account. Compliments, appreciation, listening, and empathy are counted as positive deposits. Negativity, criticism, condescension, insults, anger, and pulling away are withdrawals. Dr. John Gottman, in his research on marital stability, has found that the ratio of positivity to negativity that is needed for a relationship to succeed is 5 to 1. That means that for every negative interchange, there must be five positive ones in order for a marriage to thrive.

Communication style that can use some work:

"I can't believe you forgot to take out the trash again!"

Positive communication:

"I really appreciate it when you remember to take out the trash."

6. *Develop assertive communication. Don't expect your spouse to be a mind reader. Tell him what you would like in a direct and clear manner. Beating around the bush can lead to misunderstandings. Stating your needs does not guarantee that your spouse can meet them; it just greatly increases the chances that you can both feel heard, and hopefully even be heard.*

   Use "I" statements to share what you are feeling rather than attacking your partner for what he is doing that hurts you. The goal of an "I" statement is to allow you and your feelings to be heard, without putting the listener on the defensive.

Communication style that can use some work:

   "You drive like a maniac! You're going to end up getting us killed!"

Positive communication:

   "I feel scared when you drive so fast. Can you keep to the speed limit when I'm with you in the car? I would feel a lot less nervous, and I could enjoy being with you even more."

7. *Replace "but" with "and." Susan Heitler, a renowned couples therapist, suggests replacing "but" with "and" in couples communication. If you acknowledge what your spouse has said and then follow up with a "but," you are invalidating what he said. Rather than using "but," Heitler suggests using "and," which acknowledges what was said previously and adds to it.*

Communication style that can use some work:

   "I know you wanted to go out tonight, but I was too tired. You can't imagine how hard I worked today." (With this response, her tiredness invalidates his desire to go out and adds a competitive tone.)

Positive communication:

"I know you wanted to go out tonight, and I was too tired. Could we maybe take a rain check?" (My tiredness won out tonight, and I want your desire to go out to be met. Can we make a different time to do what you wanted to do also?)

8. Build trust. Mean what you say and stand by your word. Honesty is crucial in marriage. Lying erodes trust. Sometimes, if a spouse does something he is not proud of or is embarrassed about, he may be dishonest to cover it up or avoid consequences. Once you start lying, you won't know yourself what is true and what is not. When liars get caught, they create devastation where there would have been disappointment. Even if it's sometimes difficult, building a relationship on truth is a must.

Communication style that can use some work:

"I don't know what you're talking about. I was at work until midnight! And anyway, I don't have to tell you where I am every minute of the day!"

Positive communication:

"I'm sorry I came home so late. I left work at 10 o'clock and stopped by my brother to drop something off. We started talking and I just lost track of time. I should have called to let you know I would be late."

9. Timing is everything in communication. Schedule heavy discussions for a time when neither party is rushed, hungry, or tired. Erev Shabbos, right before candle lighting, is not the right time to bring up major changes you would like to make. At a quiet moment, say that there is an issue that you would like to discuss. Ask if this is a good time to talk. If your spouse

says that it's not, respect that and ask when might be a good time to discuss your concern.

Communication style that can use some work:

"Nobody ever helps me get ready for Shabbos! You have to do something! I can't take this." (This is an attack and will lead to your spouse feeling defensive, not getting you help.)

Positive communication:

"I feel very stressed before Shabbos. When can we sit down and discuss what we can do to relieve some of the pressure?" (This is a respectful, nonattacking request for assistance in developing a new strategy for making erev Shabbos more peaceful.)

10. Repair work. When you do something to hurt your spouse, apologize. Even if he also hurt you, be sure to take responsibility for your part of the situation. If you say something that you regret saying, rewind the tape. "I am sorry I said that — that's not what I meant" can heal a lot of hurt before it gets too far. Sometimes changing the topic, taking a break, or getting fresh air when things get too emotional is helpful. Be sure to come back to the issue later when you are feeling calmer.

If you show your spouse love and respect and a desire to do better and stay connected, then you are on the road to building a beautiful marriage. If you focus on the opposite, G-d forbid, then you are on your way to a lot of pain and unnecessary suffering.

Communication style that can use some work:

"I can't apologize for hurting you if you're always doing this! I can't take you seriously when you act like this. I know you're just going to do this again." (Hurt-

ing someone who hurt you back only leads to more fighting and more hurt.)

Positive communication:

"I'm sorry I raised my voice at you. True, I was pressured to finish this project for work, but there is no reason to take it out on you." (Taking responsibility for our mistakes helps us avoid making them again.)

No matter whether you are getting married younger or older, for the first time or not, these suggestions can help ensure that you build a solid foundation for a loving and respectful relationship. Try incorporating these suggestions into your marriage at whatever stage you are in. If you feel you need help implementing them, don't be embarrassed to ask a rabbi or therapist to help get you on track. Communication is something that can take work, but is well worth the effort.

And may you truly be zocheh to build a bayis ne'eman b'Yisrael!

Chapter 4

Misunderstandings and Miscommunications

We've all heard about the power of speech. Rarely is it more important than the beginning of marriage, when you don't know what your spouse means and haven't learned his tones, and you are the slightest bit oversensitive and eager to have everything perfect.

Even if this doesn't describe you to a tee, miscommunications and misunderstandings in the beginning of marriage can be hurtful, humorous, frequent, and unfortunately lasting. The main thing is to realize it takes time to get to know another person, lots and lots of time. It will also help to realize miscommunication and misunderstandings are normal in any new relationship, whether it be marriage, a new mother-in-law, a new boss, etc. What matters is not whether misunderstandings occur, but what you do with them.

How you react in a tough situation is as important to notice as is the irony of the situation itself. Strive to overcome the unintentionally hurt feelings that may arise, strive to develop healthy communications in the future, and strive to see the humor in these mishaps. Clear communication and understanding are ultimately gifts from Hashem, but the more we work on ourselves, the faster the gift comes.

Here are stories about what happens when you are in the beginning of your marriage and still trying to learn what your spouse means, and exactly how clear and specific you need to be with your spouse, and vice versa.

You'll notice that food is a central theme in all of these stories. This was not intentional. Originally I asked writers to write about a misunderstanding or a miscommunication in their first year of marriage. I didn't specify anything more than that. Ironically, every story I received on the topic of miscommunication ended up with food as its central theme.

At first I asked writers for more stories, thinking they would balance it out. More pieces came in about food. I was about to make a third attempt at calling for more stories, this time specifying "no food stories." Then I realized that if this was the theme so many women are writing about, this must be a real issue for many new brides. So I left it as is. Whether you are into food or not, you will see the lessons in each story, and you can apply them to your own situations whatever they revolve around.

Since reading these stories, I have come to think that food and nurturing and love and verbal communication are all different ways of communicating the same thing. You care enough about your spouse to try to make that person happy. I know this is the case for me. When I want to make my husband extra happy and feel extra cared for and supported, I definitely end up in the kitchen.

Good luck, ladies. Misunderstandings are often less than fun, but there is a deep satisfaction that comes with growing into a couple that does understand each other, and hopefully, it is through stories like these that we become those kinds of couples.

When Sensitivity Hurts

● *Chana Herzog*

I confess. I was acting like a high-strung wife. My husband had innocently asked me if the onion soup was supposed to be a creamy color, as he thought onion soup was usually a dark brown. I blinked slowly and swallowed, trying to hold back the tears. I couldn't. I was too hurt. I turned to face him, with despair written all over my face.

"I'm such a bad cook. I know I'm a bad cook. And I know you think I'm a bad cook!"

My husband stood there, helpless and apologetic. "Chana, you're an excellent cook! I just thought that maybe it's supposed to be more brown."

"Is your mother's more brown?" I asked, knowing the answer.

"Yes, I guess so...but you're just beginning. It takes time. Soon you'll be a pro!"

"So you're saying I'm not a pro now? There! I got you to admit it!"

"Oy vey." He sighed while pouring himself a bowl. I watched him like a hawk as he ate the soup, but to my dismay, he finished it and looked at me with a satisfied smile as if to say, "See, it's good! I ate the whole thing!"

Wallowing in my own pity, I refused to admit to myself that he liked it. "You're just trying to make me feel good," I muttered under my breath.

While we finished eating dinner, we talked about my little emotional performance. We tried to get to the bottom of the situation so that I wouldn't end up on the verge of tears before every meal.

"I just feel like I can't really get it right in the kitchen," I relayed with disappointment. "There's always something that's not perfect!"

"You know I love your food. When I tell you that something needs a little more salt, or the color looks different, I don't mean to attack your cooking at all. You're a great cook, but if I don't tell you how I like it, you'll never know. I'm just trying to help!"

"I know you are," I acknowledged. "It's just — you told me when we were dating that you really enjoy good food. I just want to live up to that. I don't want to disappoint you."

As the words slipped out of my mouth, I knew why I had been so sensitive. I was insecure about my cooking. I wanted my husband to be proud that he married the chef of the century, so I criticized and analyzed every remark, waiting to find out that he didn't think I was.

To me, an innocent comment became offensive because in my head I made it that. I never spent time in the kitchen as a girl, but within a few weeks of being married, I wanted everything to be gourmet on the first try. This unrealistic expectation I set for myself just made me get easily insulted.

There's a famous Chassidic story of a man who visited his Rebbe complaining that people were always offending him. He whined of constantly being verbally and emotionally attacked and asked the Rebbe what he could have done to deserve such treatment. The Rebbe wisely responded, "Maybe if you stop spreading yourself all over the place, people will stop stepping on you!"

I couldn't help thinking about that story. If you, or me in this instance, trace the steps back to the situations where we're offended by somebody else's words, and we are honest with ourselves, most likely the problem stems from our own *insecurities. We feel pained when someone touches our most vulnerable sore spots. True, sometimes people can be nasty and callous, but isn't that their problem? Why should we give a tactless remark the time of day?*

Could it be that we are so wound up because deep down the person criticizing us has brought an insecurity to the surface? That can be hard to face, but harder than that is the ability to rise above our sensitivity and realize when we are overreacting. Perhaps we are offended because we know that we have an issue we have to deal with, and putting the blame and anger on somebody else is just easier.

It is strenuous being the spouse of a person with countless insecurities. Being in a relationship with that person means that you are constantly treading on thin ice and any meaningless comment can result in disaster. It means that a compliment to somebody else in your spouse's presence arouses jealousy and suspicion. It means that a harmless joke isn't laughed at, but rather dissected and overanalyzed. It means that a remark with the intention of constructive criticism becomes an assault on his or her personality. These insecurities are time bombs waiting to explode; all you have to do is press the wrong button.

I didn't want to be that kind of person, and more importantly, I definitely did not want to be that kind of wife. So I put my pride aside, and I found a new onion-soup recipe. This one called for teriyaki sauce, which would definitely give that brown color I was looking for. I undersalted the soup and waited for my husband to come home, so that we could spice it just the way he liked it.

I prepared myself for the worst, but decided that if it didn't come out the way I wanted, I would laugh it off. I made an effort not to scrutinize his facial expressions or keep tabs on how much was left in his bowl. This isn't just about the soup, I told myself. This is about me being an easygoing, confident, and lighthearted wife.

We had fun over dinner. And the soup, I must admit, was delicious.

The Charcoal Pita

● Yiska Cohen*

We must have been married for about a month and a half. My husband said he wanted to heat a pita in our new microwave. Growing up, he had never used a microwave. His mother didn't think they were healthy, so they had a toaster oven for dairy. He asked me what to do. I'd grown up with a microwave as a central appliance, so I said, "Just stick it in the microwave and turn the dial."

Ten minutes later, I smelled smoke. I don't mean a candle going out; I mean somebody call 911, or in Israel, where we lived, call 102.

I started screaming. "Moshe! Moshe, the house is on fire! We have to get out of here!"

I heard nothing. Where is he? Thoughts raced through my mind. Which way should I run? Should I look for him or put out the fire?

I ran toward the kitchen. Black smoke filled the room, and the smell was overwhelming. In the corner of the room I saw metallic sparks flying across the counter. It was the microwave. It had to be. Though I am normally good in a crisis, this time I was clueless.

My new husband appeared from the back room, where he'd been looking something up in a sefer. "What's wrong?" he asked in utter disbelief. In a moment of Hashem's chesed, the microwave gave a ding and suddenly the sparks stopped.

I realized there was no fire, only a microwave with tinfoil in it. We carefully opened the microwave to find a tiny piece of charcoal the size of a donut hole inside, surrounded by a piece of aluminum foil.

"What was that?" I asked.

"My pita," he said innocently.

I couldn't imagine how long it had to have been in the microwave to shrink to the size of a small ball. "Moshe, how long did you turn on the microwave for?"

Moshe smiled. "I don't know, five minutes. You said turn the dial, so I did."

I couldn't decide if I should laugh or cry, but the smoke was overwhelming on either account, so we had to open all of the doors and windows. It was that day I realized just how much we still had to learn about each other.

In marriage, there are so many things you can take for granted. To me a microwave was a known entity. For my husband, it made sense to stick the pita in for five minutes because that was how long it would have taken in a toaster oven. It sounds silly, but it is metaphorical: there are so many things in life that are givens for one person, but the other partner approaches it differently.

My husband was raised frum, so for him davening and asking Hashem for what you need in life is second nature. For me, as a ba'alas teshuvah, davening is work. I always think I have to do everything on my own. I have learned to take an example from my husband's davening and realize it's O.K. for me to do the same and ask for what I really need.

In marriage, there will be many misunderstandings. Hopefully, they won't end up causing a fire in your kitchen, but sometimes they are as easy to put out as waiting for the microwave to ding and the smoke to clear so you can see what's going on.

Anniversaries 101

● Esther Grossman*

I quickly diced the cherry tomatoes and tossed them over the shredded iceberg lettuce. I was glad that I had finally found a use for this extremely colorful earthenware bowl. The colors — orange and turquoise — matched my mother's flamboyant taste perfectly.

I remembered what my mother said when she gave it to me. "It's modern and in. I thought it was perfect since you said you needed a salad bowl." I had smiled politely and thanked my mother for her terrific choice, but all I could think about was its gaudiness and impracticality.

Esther, get back to the task at hand, a voice called, pulling me away from my thoughts. I had to move fast. I wanted tonight to be special as it was our six-month anniversary. Yitzy would be back soon from kollel, and I didn't want him to find me cutting up vegetables for the salad. I wanted to be all ready, waiting with my makeup and sheitel on. It would be perfect. Then I would give him the card and poem I had written.

"Now, where is that milchig Caesar-salad dressing recipe that Shira gave me at my shower?" I muttered. "Oh, here it is."

Sometimes I talked to myself. It was one of those things that took my husband by surprise. He didn't understand how I thought talking out loud to myself was normal. Yitzy had made it known that he didn't particularly like it, but slowly he was getting used to it.

I read the ingredients from the cookbook my friends had made for me, The Grossman Family Cookbook, in honor of my new last name. "Let's see, you need to get mayo, sour cream, lemon juice, and fresh garlic out of the fridge."

I reached for a bowl and mixed in the ingredients as instructed in the recipe. While I was looking for the garlic-flavored croutons, I heard a key turning in the door.

"I'm late!" I cried. "Quick, put the garlic bread in the oven."

Yitzy opened the door and walked straight into the kitchen. I quickly took off my apron and started straightening my clothing. "Esther, what did you say? Something about bread? Did you ask me to buy bread on my way home?"

I smiled. "Oh, it was nothing important. You know me, talking to myself again." I almost missed Yitzy's eyes rolling.

"Welcome home, Yitzy. I'm sorry that everything isn't ready. I was hoping to change into my sheitel before you came home. I wanted everything to be perfect for tonight." I was so disappointed with myself and what I felt was my lack of capabilities.

"Esther, don't worry about it. Everything smells great and you look very nice in this snood. You don't need to wear your sheitel. I like coming home and seeing that you're comfortable."

I looked up and smiled widely into Yitzy's eyes. He was trying so hard to reassure me that all my efforts had not gone to waste. I really appreciated it. I suddenly felt as though a huge burden had been lifted from my shoulders.

"Thanks for understanding, Yitzy. I made something very special for tonight's menu. All of your favorites — lasagna, garlic bread, and Caesar salad. And we have milchig strawberry ice cream for dessert."

"Wow, thanks, Esther. You really outdid yourself. But...what's the special occasion?"

My head jolted upward, and I looked into Yitzy's eyes to see if he was making some kind of a joke. His blank gaze quickly informed me that he was actually clueless.

"You can't be serious. You honestly don't know what today is?"

I was hurt and deflated. I had been planning this for the past week. I was anticipating this special evening together, thinking that Yitzy was doing the same, and now he didn't even know the significance of tonight. It was all too much for me to internalize.

Yitzy shook his head, checked the date on his watch, and looked up, still puzzled.

"I thought we spoke about this last week," I said, trying to mask my disappointment by speaking more quietly and slowly.

Yitzy grabbed his chin with his right hand and stroked it. He was looking straight at the floor, while my tears formed and started falling unchecked. My eyes became unfocused, and I felt embarrassed to be crying just because Yitzy hadn't remembered the significance of today's date.

Yitzy looked crestfallen when he saw my tears. "Esther, what's the matter? I know that I forgot something important, but please don't cry. I honestly do not remember what we spoke about. I'm sorry, but if you tell me I'll remember and we can fix this all up."

His eyes were pleading with me, and I realized that he really had totally forgotten.

I remembered my kallah teacher telling me once how men don't know what to do when their wives cry, and it really hurts because they feel totally helpless. I didn't mean to hurt Yitzy, but the tears started to fall even faster. As much as I tried to stop them for Yitzy's sake, they continued to roll down my face. I was happy now that I hadn't had enough time to put on my makeup before Yitzy came home. Otherwise, I would have had black smudges under my eyes from the mascara and eyeliner. I would have looked awful.

My voice broke as I bawled, "Yitzy, it's our six-month anniversary."

"Esther, please sit down and take these tissues," Yitzy said, pulling out a kitchen chair with one hand and searching for some tissues from his pocket with the other. "Please stop crying. I didn't mean to make you so sad. I especially didn't mean to make you cry."

I sat down and blew my nose.

"Don't people normally only celebrate their full-year anniversaries? I didn't realize that six months was such a big thing."

Yitzy sounded so logical and so male at that moment. I realized right then that he had no idea how our conversation the other day had affected me. Here I had been planning a six-month anniversary to celebrate this momentous occasion, thinking we were both in on it together, when he hadn't even known what I wanted from him.

I dabbed a tissue at the corners of my eyes and nose and said, "Yes, Yitzy, you're right. But don't you remember last week when we were eating dinner Tuesday night? You had mentioned that the weeks were slipping by since we first got married. And then I reminded you that in one week we would be married for six months."

"Yes, I do remember that conversation. But how did you get the idea that I was planning to celebrate our six-month anniversary?"

"You're not getting it, Yitzy. Shouldn't this day mean something to you, too?" I was making an effort to hold back another onslaught of tears. "I thought that if you cared about our anniversary, then you would know how I'm feeling."

"I do care, Esther. Believe me when I say that. If you would have told me what you were planning, then I would have realized how important today meant to you."

How could Yitzy not know how I felt about this? If he loved me, then he would be able to understand me completely. And what? a voice of logic suddenly called out in my head. Read your mind?

Right then and there, the absurdity of my thinking and unrealistic expectations hit me. How was Yitzy to know that our six-month anniversary meant so much to me if I didn't actually tell him? It's true we discussed the event, but I never told him that it was such a milestone and that I wanted to celebrate it. He didn't know how I felt about today and that's why he didn't do anything. It had nothing to do with him not caring about me.

Suddenly, a huge smile appeared on my face and I said, "Yitzy, you are absolutely right."

He looked stunned. He had no idea what had just happened in my head. One minute I was crying, and the next minute I was smiling at him, all the hurt in my eyes gone. His eyes beckoned to me to explain what he had missed.

"I'm so sorry. I suddenly realized while we were talking that you can't read my mind and it was foolish of me to think you could."

"Esther, let's make a deal. From now on, whenever you think of anything that I should know about, you tell me out loud just to make sure we're on the same page. Even if you think it's something so obvious that I should know about it. This way I'll always be in tune with your thinking and hopefully this will never happen again. I will make a point of remembering what you tell me and try to make it as important to me as it is to you."

"Yitzy, that's a great idea. It's a deal."

"And, Esther, don't worry about our first anniversary, I learned enough from this incident that I will be sure to remember."

We both laughed, happy to have worked this issue out. Now our six-month anniversary not only signified the amount of time that had elapsed from our wedding, but also the time when we reached a deeper understanding of each other in our relationship.

Sushi, Peanut Sauce, and Other Lessons in Building a Marriage
— Beth Shapiro

Today, it wouldn't be surprising to see sushi at a bris. But back in the 1970s sushi was unheard of in the U.S. — well, almost. They served sushi at my husband's bris. That's the kind of family he came from. My mother-in-law not only has special, intricate recipes for every occasion; she also has a designated serving platter for each and every special recipe because presentation is part of the experience.

My mom, on the other hand, grew up in a New York City apartment with a galley kitchen that could fit only one person at a time. My grandmother served "meat," or what she called "food," for dinner. Mom learned to cook from my father's mother, a Polish balebusta, who taught her to make my father's favorite meals: fricassee, stuffed cabbage, and meatballs. Growing up, we had five spices in the house: salt, pepper, garlic powder, onion powder, and paprika.

When Simcha and I got married, I never really thought much about the kitchen part of being a wife. As a single person, when I got hungry I made something: a bowl of cereal, some macaroni and cheese, perhaps a frozen dinner. Or I bought something. I had a system: bagel and coffee every morning on the way to work, soup in a cup for lunch, whatever my roommate made for dinner.

It wasn't that I didn't know how to cook. I was very functional in the kitchen when I wanted to be. Even when I was single, I loved to host Shabbos meals for my friends. I would make a list, buy all the ingredients, and set aside an afternoon to make a gourmet menu, usually something involving beef or chicken in a rich sauce.

Now here I was, married, and suddenly there was this man in the house with me and he wanted to eat real food — every day. To make matters worse, he was a quirky eater. You see, at the time of our marriage, when we were still growing in Yiddishkeit, Simcha was a vegan — most simply explained, a vegetarian who didn't eat dairy or eggs. That meant no meat and no dairy. His entire diet was pareve. It consisted mostly of beans and vegetables mixed with strange spices.

Simcha was more than happy to prepare food for himself. He had spent a lot of time with his brother-in-law, one of the best chefs in the United States. But despite my mother's lack of culinary skills and my lack of cooking motivation, I came from a very traditional home. And just like my mother, who learned how to cook exactly what my father liked, if I was going to be the wife it was my job to cook, even if Simcha was better at it, and even if I hated it.

"Simcha," I would ask sweetly in the morning, "what would you like for dinner tonight?"

And he would answer something like, "I would love some palak paneer."

Then I would stare at him blankly as he explained, "It's an Indian dish with spinach, ginger paste, garlic paste, cumin, fenugreek leaves, and garam masala."

"Oh," I would reply weakly, not wanting him to know that I had no idea what any of those ingredients were. "Is there anything else?"

"Maybe a curry dish." He would pause. "Or a dal? Oh, I really like pad thai."

And then I would mention the most exotic dish I knew how to make, a dish that no one in the history of my family had ever dared to make — noodles with peanut sauce. And he would smile and say, "That sounds wonderful."

I would go out and buy the ingredients to make the dish. I'd place it on the table expectantly, and Simcha would make a berachah, taste it, and smile. "Mmmm, this tastes delicious," he'd say. "It's really good." Then he would take a few more bites and say, "You know what I really love in peanut noodles? Coconut milk."

And I would run out of the room crying because I had never even heard of coconut milk.

During shanah rishonah, we ate out a lot. We would go out to a restaurant and I would watch what he ordered. Then I would return home and try to duplicate it. I learned all about different kinds of olive oil and different kinds of vinegar. I learned about seitan (textured vegetable protein) and tofu.

One erev Shabbos I was in the kitchen rolling dough in an attempt to make homemade whole-wheat puff pastry since he didn't really like white flour — or sugar, for that matter — so that I could make tuna knishes, when he walked in smiling.

"Would you like me to show you a really good way to roll that so it's even?" he asked.

Once again, I ran out of the room crying. He was dumbfounded.

I had heard him say, "Your food is not good — you are an unworthy wife," when he, coming from a family where cooking was a group activity, was actually saying, "How exciting to have someone to share a life with. I want to talk to you and build our home together with you."

Had I heard him correctly, I might have been able to respond, "Dear Simcha, I am nervous about my role in the kitchen. When I'm called upon to do something that I am insecure about, I am so critical of myself that I need your unwavering support. Please support me unconditionally so that I can have space to grow."

I'd love to say that we sat down and talked about the problem and then came to some wonderful conclusion. I'd love to say we made menus and looked up new recipes together and learned about each other's families of origin. But it didn't happen quite like that. Life doesn't always tie up so nicely.

Simcha could see that his presence in the kitchen caused me a lot of stress. So he decided to go away. Just like that, one day he said, "This is not good for us. I'm stepping out. You're in charge of the kitchen. I'm not going to cook anything for six months. Whatever you cook, I will eat and I will like."

Then I found out I was expecting and I got sick. I was so sick that I could barely enter the kitchen. I certainly had no energy to worry about things like palak paneer. I learned that if I was going to be an effective wife, I was going to have to quit trying to be an impressive wife and move into my most basic mode: noodles and sauce, vegetable soup, rice with tofu. That's what I cooked when I could muster the energy. And when I couldn't, we ate peanut butter and honey on whole wheat bread or he ate at yeshivah. Simcha ate what I gave him and smiled, because really he had never been unhappy.

And eventually, over time, we both changed. My repertoire in the kitchen expanded. Little by little, I learned *confidence. I learned that you can make fancy recipes in a simple way, and no one will know the difference. I learned that I don't like Indian food, but I am willing to use curry. I learned that you don't have to cook like it's Shabbos on a Tuesday, and if one Shabbos you need to cook a really simple meal, everyone will understand and the food can still be delicious.*

Simcha gave up on being a vegan. He started eating dairy, not that I asked him to. And as he grew in Torah observance, he slowly began to recognize the spiritual significance of eating meat on Shabbos until one day he actually requested it.

Today, ordinary people consider me an "exotic" cook because I have a cabinet filled with spices, and I can manage to put together a full meal when our organic vegetarian friends come for Shabbos. Some days we eat chicken and other days we eat lentils. Sometimes Simcha cooks, and I don't even feel guilty anymore because I have realized that he enjoys it. His food is always spicier than mine. He keeps a little bottle of s'chug (the Middle Eastern version of hot sauce) in the refrigerator that we all know is his. I am still happiest with a good steak and mashed potatoes with an iceberg lettuce salad. But if anyone is interested, I have a really fantastic, quick recipe for coconut curry tofu soup.

One of the most important things I learned from this experience is that shanah rishonah is not your entire marriage. You don't have to get all of your emotional life baggage worked out. You couldn't if you tried. You and your spouse are coming from two different worlds, and each of those worlds has a language. "Simple dinner" in Simcha's house and "simple dinner" in my house didn't look, or for that matter taste, the same. So when we thought we were communicating, we weren't. This has been the cause of so many misunderstandings.

So when your spouse, who is usually a normal person, suddenly says something completely insane, take it as a sign that maybe, just maybe you didn't understand what he actually said. And when you suddenly feel like you cannot believe you are married to someone who could think such a thought, maybe you didn't understand correctly.

In our quest to build our relationship, Simcha and I constantly need to learn about how to navigate the changing dynamics of each other's inner worlds. We had to learn how to offer criticism with love, when not to criticize, when to support, and when to try and fix the problem, when to give space, and when to draw closer. It is a delicate balance, one that we don't always master. The important thing is that we are committed to the journey.

Chapter 5

How to Fight Right

I remember considering going to a *shiur* in my *shanah rishonah* on "How to Fight Right" and thinking, *I will never need advice on fighting. We will live to make each other happy. We will never fight. We will always resolve our differences in a civil way and never have the need for a shalom bayis shiur.*

In the end, I decided to go to meet other *kallah*s as I was in a new city and knew very few people. But it turned out that the *rebbetzin* who delivered the *shiur* was giving helpful advice on communication and how to resolve conflicts and differences of opinions in marriage. That made sense to me, as in every marriage there will eventually be disagreements. I walked away from the *shiur* inspired. My new marriage was an opportunity to learn a deeper level of communication and understanding of both my new husband and myself.

Perhaps there is an inherent issue with the word *fight*, which can be misleading. But in some situations, it is accurate. I think it can very much depend on the personalities involved and how their individuality meets when they are in conflict.

When I started researching this chapter, I had a very interesting experience. When I asked newlyweds to write, there was no problem getting stories. But when I asked older women to write of their experiences and wisdom on the subject, women who on average had been married for over thirty years, they all responded with the same answer. "We really don't fight," most of them shared. "I don't have anything to offer on the subject."

When I pushed the issue, asking the question again of women in one of my writing classes, all over fifty years old, they were horrified at my idea for the chapter's title. "'Fight' shouldn't be in the title," they said. "If you say 'fight' in the title, there's already a problem."

"How can you say that?" I asked. "You never fight with your spouse?"

"No," they unanimously agreed. Then they went on to share their experiences with their husbands and how they dealt with each other when conflicts arose in their marriages.

I left the conversation inspired and uplifted, as well as slightly flabbergasted and questioning my ideas on the chapter. I continued my research and came to find what I think is the dividing line between newlyweds and couples who have been married for many years. The women of the generations before ours all said that in marriage it's a "give-and-give," and thus they had harmonious lives and marriages. The challenges I expected them to write about simply didn't exist. Each partner gave what the other needed, and they had little or no conflict.

I, too, had heard the idea that marriage is about "give-and-give"; it's something all *kallah*s are taught. And yet, in my own life and in the lives of many young women I know, I have often seen moments when it's easier to quote the idea than to live it. Time has complicated the role of marriage and the roles each spouse is expected to perform.

One of the women I asked to offer her thoughts on marriage made a cute but accurate joke. She said, "In this generation, we all expect instant marriage, just add water. A good marriage isn't like that. It's something you work on forever to keep good and make better."

In the Torah, we have many examples of our holy *Avos* and *Imahos* working hard to resolve important issues in their lives. There are many moments in the Torah when our forefathers and foremothers could have given up but chose to work harder to get their desired results. Yaakov Avinu wrestled all night with an angel and emerged victorious. Avraham Avinu negotiated with Hashem over saving the people of Sedom. Moshe Rabbeinu begged 515 times to be blessed to enter the Land of Israel. Rivkah Imeinu went for counsel when she thought the "child" she was carrying pulled her both toward the house of study and the house of *avodah zarah*. And Leah's eyes were weak from crying and davening for a higher-level soul mate than Esav.

All of these examples display that we have a long history in our spiritual tradition of working hard to resolve conflicts, inner or outer. Sometimes a negotiation is needed; sometimes a spiritual wrestling match occurs: what can feel like wrestling with an issue can be both holy and spiritually important.

I once heard a marriage therapist say that when a couple that didn't fight at all came to her for help, they were in the worst shape of all. It was only the marriages that people fought for, once they were having trouble, that lasted.

At first I thought that didn't make any sense. She explained that "fighting means you care enough to get upset, to confront an issue, that in a way it means you believe enough in the union to work on it." She continued by saying, "The marriages that, G-d forbid, end are most often the ones that neither party is willing to fight for. Again, read 'fight' as resolve differences, work on issues, learn to communicate better."

In this chapter, I have included stories from women married less than ten years. For a completely different take on fighting, see the chapter on advice from wise women in which I asked women married much longer to speak about when they "fight." When I write about women married over thirty years, you'll be amazed at the perspectives you'll find and the effect time can have on a relationship.

If you are in *shanah rishonah*, and you have never considered the idea of having a difference of opinion and the idea of fighting doesn't enter your mind, be grateful to Hashem. But if you have dealt with any level of difference of opinion, conflict, or even an actual fight, read on and see if any of these stories help you on your journey to the best marriage you can possibly have.

May we all be *zocheh* to be married for many years to come, and be able to help all women in their new marriages with the advice, wisdom, and life experiences we have gained.

Making Sure Neither of Us Comes Out the Loser

───────────────────────────────── • *Rochel Boyde*

As I look back at my shanah rishonah, which was almost at its end when I wrote this, the one thing I regret is how many fights it took to get to the peace and stability my husband and I now enjoy. It's easy when you're newly engaged or newly married to assume that you and your intended will never fight. Let me tell you, my husband is my best friend and he is the best friend I have ever had. We share many of the same values, interests, and priorities. Not a day goes by that I don't thank Hashem for bringing us together. I know how blessed I am to be married to such a wonderful, intelligent, and good man. And still we fight. Not often. Not violently. But still, it happens.

It's normal — and natural — to argue with the people closest to you. In my opinion, there are two types of arguments: ones that emanate from bad moods and ones that result from actual circumstances. As far as I'm concerned, it's not O.K. to pick a fight with someone (especially someone you love) just because you're having a bad day. It is, however, O.K. to disagree with someone when you take issue with his words or actions.

Most things aren't worth causing an argument, so we've learned how to pick our battles. It drives me batty when my husband leaves half-read books on every available surface in our apartment. But it takes me less time to pick them up and put them away than it does to fight about it. My husband can't stand that I leave empty water glasses everywhere. But it takes him less time to move them to the sink where I'll inevitably wash them that day than it does to complain. In the end, our efforts even out. We both have the opportunity to appreciate what the other does for us, and we don't have to waste energy arguing over trivialities.

I'm not suggesting that you never raise concerns. There are plenty of times when you should raise legitimate issues with your spouse. When I swallow problems and keep them bottled up, it does not end well. In fact, it tends to result in an explosion of emotion on my unsuspecting husband who — until that moment — had no reason to suppose anything was amiss. We've learned that it is necessary to discuss and deal with real problems before they snowball into out-of-control fights, to try, as calmly and rationally as we can (it's O.K. to give yourself time to cool off before a discussion), to explain our perspectives to each other. One thing my legal education taught me is that it's much harder to argue with facts and logic than it is with emotion.

In the first few fights we had, we both viewed proving our point as our number-one priority. Afterward we realized that we still had to live with each other; no matter how many mean comments we had lobbed in each other's direction. It's devastating when a fight is over and peace reigns to realize that you can't always soothe those wounds. You might have fought each other to a standstill, or you might genuinely have agreed on a solution, but either or both of you has been hurt, embarrassed, or had his or her confidence shattered.

There is a huge difference between telling someone that his words are mean and telling him that he is mean. Point out specific behavior that you don't like. It's O.K. to tell your spouse how you would have liked him to say something to you. During one fight, my husband told me that I didn't care about him. I became even more incensed than I previously had been because I felt like he was accusing me of something that wasn't true. We finally agreed that he should have said, "Right now I feel like you don't care about me." Saying it that way doesn't make me feel like a bad person, and it doesn't put me on the defensive. Rather, it helps me see our interactions through his eyes; and it helps me realize that I don't want him to feel like that. The burden becomes mine to show him that, of course, I care. And I'm willing to examine myself and my actions to prove it to him.

It took us months to understand that 90 percent of our fights started as minor misunderstandings. But once an argument starts to escalate, it's really difficult to step back and ask what it is that you're really fighting over. Words get said (or shouted) during fights that aren't easy to take back. Within a marriage, you can confuse and anger your spouse with your silence or actions. But it is your words that can truly hurt the person you love.

Many years ago, I read a book by Rabbi Dr. Abraham J. Twerski in which he writes that in a fight there is a winner and a loser. If you are the winner, then naturally the other person is the loser. When it is your spouse you are fighting with, in order to win you must make the person you love lose. I don't care what the issue is; there is nothing so important to me that I'm willing to turn my husband into a loser. He, in turn, feels the same about me. Judaism teaches us that a married couple is like one person, so when you make your spouse out to be a loser, you are also making yourself out to be one.

We aren't afraid to end a fight. During the biggest (read: loudest, longest, and most cringe-worthy) fight my husband and I ever had, we understood that there was no easy resolution. We realized that the argument had escalated far beyond where it had started. We knew that our emotions and our relationship were on seriously unstable ground. And we knew that we loved each other and didn't want to keep fighting. So we stopped. We both agreed to put down our proverbial swords and stop hurting each other. An hour later, we got dressed up, went out, and had a wonderful date night.

Unfortunately, we didn't figure all this out right away. Today, I'm proud to say, even though we still disagree at times, we rarely ever fight for longer than a few minutes. It's amazing what the words, "I love you and I respect your opinion. I just happen to see things differently. Please let me explain," can do for your marriage.

Everyone fights. No one likes it, and no one expects it to happen to her. The truth is, it happens and it isn't necessarily anyone's fault. Sometimes fights will strengthen your relationship — perhaps by giving you the stability that comes from knowing your marriage can weather rough patches. Sometimes fights will threaten to break your bond. However, if in the heat of an argument you can remember that your marriage is your number-one priority, you most likely will be able to recognize that whatever you are fighting about is not worth ruining your marriage. I can tell you with absolute certainty that nothing is worth destroying mine.

My Top Five Tips for Fighting Right:

1. Speak to your spouse as an adult. He is not your child; don't treat him like one.

2. Don't bring up past wrongs; it will only muddle the problem at hand and dredge up old pain.

3. Remember that your goal is not to win; it's to problem-solve.

4. Confide in a mentor or older friend if necessary, but do not air your dirty laundry in public.

5. Keep in mind that your common goal is a healthy, happy, and successful marriage. Don't let anger undermine that goal.

Which Buttons Are Really Being Pushed?

Devorah Frank*

As a child, I hated fighting. I hated the idea that two adults would go head-to-head about anything. What could be that important? I wondered. I remembered various adults I knew fighting, loud voices, and the pain their words caused, and decided that I would never fight with anyone that way. I was 100 percent sure I would never be like that.

And then my turn came to marry. I will never forget our first fight. It was really just a misunderstanding that turned into a disagreement. By the time it was over, it felt like a fight.

My husband went to the store to buy milk. He came home and started to unload the groceries. The actual conversation went like this:

Husband: "I brought home the groceries."

Me: "Honey, thank you so much for shopping. By the way, I prefer milk in a carton, not a bag. It stays fresher longer. Do you mind getting the milk in a carton next time?"

Husband: "It's just milk. I don't know why you're making such a big deal out of this."

Me: "I am not making a big deal out of anything. I just want a different kind of milk."

From the look on his face, I knew I'd just made a major mistake. To me, it was a simple request. To him, he'd just been shot with an arrow. How could I criticize him like that? How could I not appreciate what he had just done?

That incident led to our first fight. We didn't yell. We didn't use loud voices, but it was clear he felt dejected. And it was because of me. How could I? I felt confused. What had I done? In my eyes, I'd made a simple request. I learned later from a discussion with him that he felt I was invalidating his ability to make decisions for our family. I had unintentionally hurt him. I have learned that men and women are different, and the way a man and a woman see the same issue may have absolutely nothing to do with reality.

If I were a different person, had read more psychology, and was less assertive, maybe I would have just said sorry and avoided a conflict. But I couldn't leave well enough alone.

Instead of simply apologizing, I invalidated him. I told him I really didn't understand what the big deal was, it had nothing to do with him, and he absolutely wasn't being criticized. I didn't stop there. I continued into territory in which a good wife should never venture. I said that this whole thing was being blown out of proportion, that he should be happy that I told him what I wanted so he could make me happy. Wasn't that the point of marriage: to make each other happy? What was the big deal? Couldn't he just get different milk?

Through this incident and our later discussions, I later understood the words under the surface that weren't spoken.

Him: "I brought home the groceries." I did something praiseworthy. Compliment me. (Growing up I didn't get as much attention for positive actions as I needed.)

Me: "I prefer milk in a carton, not a bag." Through his childhood baggage (wound) he heard: I'm not good enough. I never get anything right. She doesn't think I'm competent. She doesn't think I can do anything right.

Him: "It's just milk. I don't know why you're making such a big deal out of this." Through my childhood baggage (wound) of Nobody listens to me, I heard: Your opinion doesn't matter. Why are you such a critical, overbearing wife?

I felt invalidated for my request and hurt that he didn't care about making me happy. Those feelings turned into anger. Why did it matter if I liked different milk? Why couldn't we get both? I felt attacked.

As I wrote this piece, it hurt. I am embarrassed by the incident, but now, after gaining deeper insight into what was really going on, I understand us as a couple so much better.

Part of the work in marriage is learning about each other's childhood baggage and wounds and how to be the most supportive, helpful, and understanding spouse we can be.

I often see this with couples who have the same fights happen over and over. When you realize you're always fighting about the same issue, there is a lesson to be learned. Your buttons are being pushed for a reason, and so are his. I once heard someone say, "You can't allow others to push your buttons. You have to be in charge of your own buttons."

I remember walking out of the room thinking, Nice idea. Now how do you do it? I realize now that it's more than simply not allowing your buttons to get pushed; it's identifying why your buttons are your buttons. Why something that makes you want to cry or scream can roll off your spouse's back without a thought or vice versa.

The real question is why these are your buttons and how you diffuse them so they aren't so sensitive. If my button is "feeling heard," then every time I make a request of my husband that isn't acted upon, I don't simply think, He's busy, he'll get to it later. I hear, I don't hear you. Your needs aren't important to me.

Baruch Hashem, I have an incredibly loving and devoted husband, so in my conscious mind I know that is simply not true or how he feels. But through my own childhood wounds, I sometimes experience his actions in a way he doesn't intend.

I am amazed at how much we bring into marriage unwittingly. There is so much more going on inside each of us than we see on the surface. We are each so much more than we think we are. On many levels, we are starting a new life together. On other levels, marriage is about tikkun, rectification, and you are paired with your spouse not only to love and support each other but also to be pushed to fix the parts of yourself that need to be healed. With this idea in your consciousness, it is natural that conflicts will arise, as they are opportunities for growth.

Working through conflict is often challenging. But any couple who is experiencing any level of conflict in their relationship might want to consider which of their buttons are being pushed and what is going on beyond the words that are spoken.

Fight for Survival

●— Sara Mayer*

I learned pretty early on that there are bound to be disagreements.

"What do you mean you only use that brand of toothpaste?"

"How can you store the peanut butter in the fridge?"

"Do you really insist on hospital corners on the sheets every morning?"

We grew up in different homes with different families and different life experiences. Some things just weren't going to mesh right away. The shocker was that some of these things were going to be bigger than a dispute over toothpaste brands.

"Why must we spend yom tov again with your family?"

"No, I absolutely don't approve of you taking that class."

"What is wrong with that job? It's better than nothing."

As we attempted to navigate our way through shanah rishonah, we spent most of our time avoiding the land mines. It seemed like the best idea. What could be better than a marriage without fighting? He agreed to store the peanut butter in the pantry, and I discovered that his brand of toothpaste prevented cavities in much the same way mine did. Anything bigger was circumvented or ignored. Better to push it under the rug than to deal with it. Right?

Wrong.

I have heard that often the marriages that are in the greatest danger of falling apart are those that have no disagreements at all. To an outsider, everything looks rosy. The couple is always smiling. They speak politely to each other. The neighbors never hear them raise their voices. In other words, the couple is doomed.

Six months into our marriage, I took a peek under the rug and recoiled at what I saw. The issues weren't going away. They were actually getting bigger and had started to grow horns. In our eagerness to avoid fighting, we had begun to avoid communication altogether. Sure, we discussed the parashah at the Shabbos table. We wished each other good-bye before leaving the house, and I dictated the shopping list to him every Wednesday. But something was missing: the real deep conversation that makes any relationship work.

Afraid of where we were heading, I did what any wife would do: I insisted my husband take me out to dinner.

Once at the restaurant — neutral and very public grounds — I was able to start my conversation.

"We need to talk."

My husband crossed his arms and sighed. "What did I do wrong?"

I shook my head. "No, you misunderstood me. We need to talk."

"About what?"

"Everything."

Then he understood. Or at least he made a good effort at pretending to understand. The issue in our situation was that we spent all our time avoiding the situation. If we just hashed it out, we would get over the hurdles a whole lot easier. And as a team!

Disagreeing means something different for every couple. For those who have perfected their middos, it may mean sitting at the table politely discussing all the angles. For my husband and me, it sometimes entails raised voices and passionate opinions. Whatever works best for the couple, the outcome is still the same: getting the issue out in the open will prevent it from festering under the rug.

Today my husband and I try to set aside time every day just to talk. Sometimes we end up discussing the weather, but when there is a problem we hash it out until a solution that works for both of us is found. We are working on building a healthy marriage and see "fighting" as the spice that makes any relationship worthwhile.

The Art of Arguing

● Aviva Kaufman

We enter a favorite café on one of those rare evenings out.

"Where do you want to sit?" he asks.

"The booth in the corner." I have learned to choose my words deliberately rather than just blurt out the automatic "I don't know, wherever you want."

As we make our way through the restaurant, he nods to a different booth. "Last time we sat there. Remember what happened? That was back when we didn't know how to argue."

I don't remember. Not the faintest recollection. It's touching that he does.

"Really? What happened? What did we argue about?"

"I remember it was very unpleasant. All the things we've learned not to do."

He doesn't want to go into details. Thinking back, it went something like this:

"The house is messy, don't you think so?" (Me dropping a bombshell with no introduction and wanting him to agree.)

"No." (Him answering in the most precise way possible and leaving no room for further discussion.)

"What do you mean, 'No'? Your socks are everywhere, the trash is overflowing, and your books are scattered all over the table and couch." (Me attacking, overexaggerating, and taking zero responsibility — all while we're hungrily awaiting the waitress to take our order.)

"There's no room in the laundry basket anyway, and your school papers are also all over the table and couch." (Him getting defensive.)

"Yeah, well, I'm the one who eventually cleans it up. You treat the house like it's a hotel. Come home, eat, go to shul, and leave a mess." Touché, but I'd lost him. He'd retreated into his cave.

We ate in silent tension. He didn't even offer me a taste of his pasta. How could he? For that matter, how couldn't he? He knew I loved tasting his food. He must be really hurt. I felt torn between guilt and frustration.

"I'm sorry," I said. "I'm overwhelmed with the housework, and I just don't know how to manage it by myself. I didn't mean to hurt you."

And we started to slowly rebuild.

This time we also have "issues" to discuss, but it ends with laughter and a shared ice cream — even though he doesn't like sharing food.

"I'm having a hard time with something," he starts. "Could we talk about it?"

I feel privileged that he's sharing with me rather than keeping it in. It's a sign he cares enough about our relationship to work on it.

"Sure. What are you finding difficult?" (I remind myself to listen intently without interrupting.)

"I like to be early for things. Like getting to weddings early, for instance. Being early means I don't have to work *under pressure, and I can enjoy the event. I'm also finding our erev Shabbos preparations difficult. It's very stressful to shop, cook, and clean all in one day and then bring in Shabbos tired and barely making the cutoff time."*

I had been thinking about the same thing. But between finishing school and starting a part-time job, Friday was the only day to make Shabbos. I knew I was falling short, but I was really trying.

Breathe in. Breathe out. No getting defensive. "So what you would like is to bring in Shabbos earlier and feel rested and ready in time?"

"Yes, exactly." He smiles.

"I'd love that, too. It's just that every other day of the week I have school, work, or papers to finish. So I don't start until Friday and then there never seems to be enough time."

"You have a point. You are very busy and Fridays are getting shorter." (I feel validated.) He continues. "How about we make a list of the shopping, cooking, and cleaning that needs to be done before Shabbos and split it up into little jobs throughout the week? I can pick up things on the way home from kollel, and if you have the groceries earlier you can start cooking earlier."

"O.K. I could also try to freeze things like the chicken soup. I remember my mom did that."

"And that way you won't have to make everything every week. Also, maybe we could have a cutoff time that we know we want to be finished by."

"And take naps so we don't start falling asleep at the Shabbos table. I have to be careful about not starting to clean all the big things like the fridge when I see I'm running out of time."

"That sounds reasonable. I would look forward to Shabbos much more."

The truth is that most of our arguments revolve around things that he or I would like to improve on. Admitting it to each other and even more so to ourselves is often the hard part. And actually starting the work is the harder part. After all, knowing and doing are two different parashahs. However, being able to discuss these issues in an open, productive way is the first step.

It's taken many an argument to learn the art of arguing. We're down to a few sniffles (from me), a couple of moments of silence (from him), and several lines of active listening and "I'm sorry's" (from both). The effort is conscientious and constant. We've learned to:

1. *Eat and rest, even a little. Usually sparks fly when someone is hungry or tired, especially at the end of a long day taking care of kids or coming home from work or kollel. Having dinner ready on time is a top priority.*

2. *Know each other's "hot spots" and plan ahead to avoid them. I like to leave the house clean before we go on a trip. I start washing the dishes an hour before it's time to head out. He doesn't like being pressured for time or being late (and I rarely get anywhere on time). I've learned to clean the house a day ahead and pretend we're leaving an hour earlier. He's learned to schedule in a "last-minute tidy-up" before we go.*

3. *Leave moms, dads, and any other family members out of heated moments. It's true my family doesn't need to be notified every time we arrive home safely and his side could inquire more about how things are going, but I've learned to relish the easiness of noninvolvement, and he's come to see that the overprotectiveness is just a strong sign of care and concern.*

4. *Use "I" statements and clear, specific instructions. "You only took out the trash in the kitchen. But what*

about the trash in the study and guest room? And you left the bin in the middle of the room without a trash bag and with a trail of liquid. What were you thinking?" is less effective than *"I would like the trash from the study and guest room to be emptied out with the kitchen trash. Sometimes it's easier to take the whole bin outside so as not to leave a trail. Afterward, could you please put the bin back with a clean trash bag? When the trash is taken care of, I feel taken care of, even though it sounds weird. I really appreciate it. Thanks!"*

5. *Notice patterns in our arguing. Certain times are more likely to bring out arguments. Erev Shabbos time? Erev bills-due time? Erev "off" time? Erev dinnertime? Once the pattern is noticed, it's easier to bite your tongue and realize,* It's not me or him; it's just "that time."

6. *Have a goal in mind before you start. What is my goal in bringing this up? How realistic is it? How can I best hope to achieve that goal? And how can I avoid hurting feelings on the way to achieving it?*

Chapter 6

Shanah Rishonah in Israel: Now What Do I Do for the Next Year?

Shanah rishonah is an adjustment anywhere, but if you have decided to spend your *shanah rishonah* in Eretz Yisrael, it can be even more of an adjustment. Don't get me wrong. Spending your first year in Israel is an incredible blessing. *Baruch Hashem*, my first year was spent in the Holy Land, and I am forever grateful for it. But you will have to adjust to certain things that you may have taken for granted in your country or city of origin.

The key to many a successful marriage is being flexible, and spending *shanah rishonah* in the Holy Land will offer you ample opportunity to learn flexibility, how to go with the flow, and how to adjust in many interesting ways. There will be a different accent on the Hebrew you may think you know. And the cultural differences will remind you that you aren't in New York, Baltimore, California, England, or Australia anymore. My best advice is to look at it as an adventure.

Being blessed to live in Eretz Yisrael, I have met many *kallah*s over my years here, as well as having been a *kallah* here myself. You can always tell a *kallah* in Eretz Yisrael. They are the ones glowing in the coffee shops, sipping the divinely inspired ice coffees we enjoy here. They are usually the girls with the most beautiful *sheitel*s in the most up-to-date styles. And most often they are the ones who aren't accompanied by a baby stroller when they walk through the *shuk* or grocery store.

It's a wonderful thing to watch a new *kallah* here in Israel. Her eyes are filled with hope and joy, and she is smiling. The year is filled with wonder and discovery. From how to shop to how to cook to how to fill a day in a new city in a new country you know you probably won't be staying in forever.

There is an odd reality in most *kallah*s' consciousness that the year will end, and then their real life will start once they go home. There is a feeling that you have to make the most of your time here, and yet there is so much adjusting to do that the smallest thing can feel like a big endeavor.

It is a great merit to live in Israel for any amount of time, and for those lucky enough to start their *shanah rishonah* here, I salute you. You inspire me every time I see you, and you remind me to think back to the beautiful times the first year can hold and savor those thoughts and feelings. Here are a few stories to remind you that you're not alone in what you are experiencing.

The Lucky One

————————————————————————● *Elisheva Reitzer*

I was told that I was lucky; I was told that I was someone to be envied and to grab the opportunity with both hands. When I deplaned and was actually standing on

Israeli soil, all I felt was an odd sense of misplacement, as though someone had sent me through the post and left me standing there with glazed eyes and a disoriented mind. I felt so lost, even cheated in a certain sense. I had expected upon arrival to experience the same feelings as the people in the storybooks who would bend down and kiss the soil with great reverence. Or at least to feel pleased to join in the clapping in tribute to our safe arrival. But all I wanted to do was make a U-turn.

The first week I walked around vaguely trying to appreciate the magic of Eretz Yisrael, but finding it elusive among the Hebrew lettering and manners so different from my own. I would walk into a grocery, longing to see a familiar item, anything to remind me of home, but the packages just taunted me, as if daring me to figure out what they were all supposed to be.

I slowly had to get accustomed to the welcoming squad that would come to greet me each time I neared my front door. I learned not to be scared of them. They were the cutest things, and so what if they startled me with their meows?

I had arrived at a time when the Kinneret was rapidly swelling, much to the delight of the Israeli population. There would be ongoing storms for weeks and weeks while I was left searching for the light of Eretz Yisrael. And slowly I found it. I guess it had been there all along. It lay in the nooks and crannies of Meah Shearim, in the worn-out walls of the Old City. It lay in the fact that "facing mizrach" to daven actually meant facing toward the Beis HaMikdash, as I was already in Yerushalayim. It lay in the simplicity and purity of the people, in the very stones that were trodden on by the giants of our generations and the generations of yore. The feeling of detachment finally gave way to a feeling of belonging, and suddenly I was lucky.

What a Year!

Leah Glick*

I never thought of myself as the type of girl to marry someone in learning. To be honest, I never dreamed of spending my first year of marriage in Israel either. But some things rub off on you in life without your realizing it. I have an uncle in Tzefas who has been learning for over twenty years, so I think the idea of kollel and Eretz Yisrael somehow seeped into my consciousness unintentionally.

I visited my uncle and his family every summer growing up. Though I loved my visits with them, at the time I couldn't imagine taking on the Israeli lifestyle. Each summer, people would ask me if I could see myself living here in Israel. And each year I would echo my sentiments from the year before: "I doubt it. Israeli living isn't for me."

I remember feeling it the strongest when I helped my aunt sift flour for challah. The back-and-forth motion of the sifter symbolized struggle to me. In America I just opened a bag of flour and poured it into a bowl. Here sifting flour felt like one more thing to make your life hard.

I returned to California summer after summer, simultaneously content and suffering. I missed Israel every day from August to the following June. Still, the thought of actually moving to Israel after I married and raising a family there felt like too much. I contented myself with what I thought was the best for my future. With Hashem's help, I would marry an American with a professional job and, if possible, we would continue to visit Israel in the summer.

Well, there is a saying in Yiddish that I have come to understand better and better the older I get: "A mensch tracht un G-tt lacht." Man plans and G-d laughs. That's what I had to remind myself standing in the Israeli market, in my second week of marriage, trying to figure out which sifter to buy for making challah. Apparently sifters come in different categories that mean different kashrus levels of challah. A mehadrin sifter has holes much smaller than that of one that is not mehadrin. So after making my determination, I walked out of the store, mehadrin sifter in hand.

I grew up loving the Jewish joke "What does a Jewish princess make for dinner?" The answer: "Reservations." Though I didn't grow up a card-carrying Jewish princess, I had high hopes of becoming one, in the best sense of the term, of course, once I was married. My plans of settling in Los Angeles and thinking my biggest shanah rishonah decision would be where to make reservations that night apparently were not in Hashem's plans for me.

I married an American Israeli, who would be learning full time in the Shomron. My new husband would wake up at 5:30 to take a bus to his kollel and return around 8 or 9 at night. I was proud of what he was doing, but to say I had a lot of free time on my hands would be an understatement. On one hand, there was lots of time. On the other hand, I was clueless about the new country I was living in. I needed every minute to figure out where to buy all the ingredients that went into something as simple as spaghetti and meat sauce.

I always flash back to my first attempt at preparing a homemade dinner for my husband coming back after a long day at kollel. I'd been cooking for years and was quite proficient in the kitchen. The problem was I only spoke three words of Modern Hebrew. I had once learned how to give directions to a cab driver, and *thus my entire vocabulary consisted of yeminah (right), semolah (left), and yashar (straight). You can imagine that my Hebrew vocabulary didn't translate into how to buy ingredients for spaghetti and meat sauce very well.*

As if the language barrier wasn't enough, there was the kashrus. In America, it was simple. You went into the kosher store and bought glatt kosher meat products and chalav Yisrael dairy. I didn't know that in Israel there are well over fifteen different hechsheirim on meat, and though many of them say glatt, that doesn't necessarily make them accepted by everyone.

One of the first things I did was put our Israeli rav's number on speed dial. The next thing I did was try to familiarize myself with the different hechsheirim while walking up and down the aisles of the shuk. It turns out in Israel there are also hechsheirim on fruits and vegetables, as well as extra precautions to be taken during a Shemittah year, which it was.

After a four-hour shopping trip to buy the ingredients for my simplest menu, I returned home exhausted. I unpacked the groceries and began preparing our dinner. By the time my husband arrived home at 8, there was a beautiful meal prepared and waiting for him.

We ate our dinner and spoke about each of our day's events. As we cleared the dinner dishes, my husband looked at me and said, "Thank you for the delicious dinner. Would you like to take a walk to the Kosel? It's a beautiful night."

"I'd love to," I answered.

As we walked to the Kosel, a mere twenty-minute walk from our apartment, it was suddenly clear to me exactly what I was doing here in Eretz Yisrael.

Shanah Rishonah in Israel:
How Challenges Build Character

Shoshana Bronstein*

The balance of the work-marriage dichotomy is difficult to maintain in any country. Living in Israel during our shanah rishonah, as relatively recent immigrants, presented some additional challenges for us.

For instance, a commute of one and a half to two hours is common in the United States; most families have at least one car, and spouses can expect to travel that distance if they choose to live in the suburbs of a large city. In Israel, however, such a commute is considered very difficult, and indeed proved to be.

While we were going out, I worked for a company in Rechovot's Science Park and commuted every day from Jerusalem. The ninety-minute journey each way took its toll. My workday would start at 8 a.m., when I boarded the bus from Jerusalem's Central Bus Station, and would end between 8 and 8:30 at night, when I finally arrived back in Jerusalem. Our dates would start at 9 o'clock at the earliest.

When things started to go well, our dates got longer and the amount of sleep I got each night decreased. Seeing that such a lifestyle was not sustainable, I quit my job when we got married. It wasn't exactly an easy decision, because it meant that my husband ended up being our sole breadwinner during the first five months of our marriage. However, I enjoyed spending my evenings with my husband rather than spending them sleeping or davening on an Egged bus.

We took pains to manage the financial balance. While my husband continued on with his job as a technical writer, I started Ulpan. I studied Hebrew for five hours a day, five days a week, for five months, all courtesy of the Israeli government.

I knew that going to Ulpan would be a bit of a sacrifice, since I couldn't work much while in Ulpan. My classes were free, but I didn't earn any money from them either, and we really needed the money that a job would bring. However, we both recognized that in the long term, Hebrew competence was a vital resource for me and for our future family.

Living in the United States or Canada (or any other English-speaking country), you take it for granted that your bank teller or dry cleaner will speak to you in English. In Israel, Hebrew is the language you need. The rewards of being able to ask a question in a store or reading the notes that our children would bring home from school far outweighed the immediate costs, challenging though they were.

Nevertheless, I really enjoyed my time in Ulpan. It was my best five months in Israel thus far!

Shanah rishonah has its challenges no matter where you live. We had to make some decisions that might seem odd to those who spent their shanah rishonah in the United States. But I think this is a metaphor for marriage. You have to sometimes make decisions you never thought you would make. You also have to be prepared to make some short-term sacrifices to achieve long-term goals. You have to be willing to compromise, or work a little harder, to help when your spouse is in need. But learning together and experiencing life as a team is one of the most rewarding parts of marriage.

There are certainly aspects of living in the United States that we miss, but we wouldn't trade our shanah rishonah experience in Israel for anything in the world. In fact, the challenges of living in Israel strengthened the bond between us, and we are now closer than ever.

Cheesecake

• Avigail Rudnick

"You've just got to use my cheesecake recipe," Racheli insisted. "This is your first Shavuos here, so you don't understand. You can't just use your mother's recipe from America. All the dairy products are different here. All they have is gevinah levanah, gevinah tzehubah..."

"O.K., O.K.," I said with a laugh. "So what's so special about your recipe?"

"It's a real Israeli recipe that I got from my aunt who's lived here for years," Racheli responded confidently. "But she's originally from New York, so she gets the whole 'New York cheesecake' standard that we're going for."

I smiled as I meticulously copied down the recipe. I wanted our first cheesecake, our first Shavuos, as a couple to be perfect.

Gavriel and I had gotten married in January and moved to Eretz Yisrael right after Pesach. The weather was hot, the apartment tiny, the bus rides to and from work and kollel exhausting, but we were happy. We had good friends from seminary and yeshivah living in our neighborhood. I had gotten a job in the Old City with a large nonprofit organization two weeks after we had arrived. The job came with air-conditioning and a built-in social network. Gavriel was finding his place in the Mir Yeshivah in the Beis Yisrael neighborhood. Slowly, I was learning to cook with new ingredients.

Negotiating the local makolet was a totally different experience from shopping at the Seven Mile Market in Baltimore, where we had lived for the first four months of our marriage.

"Whee-ooh, whee-ooh!"

What was that noise? Was that the Arab worker coming up behind me asking me to move?

"Geveret!"

I guess I was right! I gingerly pulled my shopping cart to one side of the aisle. The Arab squeezed past me lugging a big cardboard box. He set it down on the floor and began to unload it onto the shelves in front of me, blocking my path. I sighed and pulled my shopping cart backward, walking into someone right behind me.

"Oh, excuse me, I'm so sorry!"

I had bumped into a short woman with glasses, wearing a navy snood. Next to her was a stroller loaded with groceries. She looked up from the onions she was inspecting. "That's fine, don't worry about it."

"Actually, um, could you help me, please? I'm looking for the kind of lettuce that doesn't have bugs in it. I think it's called 'Aleh something'?"

"Oh, sure! It's right over here." She pushed her stroller around the corner and pointed to the refrigerator shelves along the wall. "Here it is." She paused, as if wondering if she should say something else. "Did you just move to the neighborhood?"

I smiled gratefully. "Yes, we just moved from Baltimore a couple of weeks ago."

She nodded knowingly. "It's a big adjustment."

"How long have you been here?"

"About ten years." Ten years! A lifetime. "You get used to it. The shopping is really different."

"Yes, I'm realizing that. Well, thank you so much. Maybe I'll see you around!" I added optimistically. It would be nice to make a new friend in this neighborhood.

I walked home in the hot sun, bags of groceries cutting into the palms of my hands. Beads of sweat formed on my nose and forehead. I can't wait to get home. We had no air-conditioning in our one-bedroom apartment, but a borrowed fan kept the worst of the heat at bay.

Shavuos came and went. The summer heat intensified. I felt tired, more tired than I'd ever been. The bus rides to and from work left me drained.

And then my suspicions were confirmed. We were expecting.

Expecting! That's supposed to be exciting. After all, we'd waited and wondered for six months. But what were we excited about? I didn't know anything about babies, and Gavriel didn't either. I'd never even changed a diaper! What would motherhood be like? How could I be excited if I didn't even know what I was excited about?

Gavriel, a father? For some reason that was an even more intriguing idea than imagining me as a mother. We both come from relatively small families; I have two sisters and Gavriel has one. None of them have children yet. I had seen Gavriel playing with our shadchan's children at our vort. He looked comfortable with them. Would we be comfortable with our own?

But between my job, commuting, and learning to cook, I didn't have too much time to worry about our future parenting skills. My schedule was demanding but enjoyable. After sharing breakfast with Gavriel, we would part ways at around 9 o'clock — he to one bus stop, I to another. My bus route wound through the neighborhoods of Ramat Eshkol, Maalot Dafna, and Arzei HaBirah before turning into East Jerusalem. I would gaze with interest through the bus's plastic windows at the Arab women doing their shopping on the crowded streets, often accompanied by their children. After an hour on the bus,

I would trudge up the steps from the Kosel to the office where I worked in the Old City.

My friends sometimes asked me if I liked working in the Old City because I had the opportunity to daven at the Kosel every day. They were surprised when I told them that since I see the Kosel every day, I'm used to it and I hardly ever daven there. A person can get used to anything, even Yerushalayim, even the Old City, even the Kosel.

Usually I got home at around 5 in the afternoon. Sometimes I went grocery shopping on the way; then I would get home closer to 6. Some nights there was barely enough time to throw something together for dinner before Gavriel came home at 7:30. After dinner, Gavriel would go out to night seder. This was my time to do the dishes and the laundry and talk to my mother on the phone.

Through the grapevine, I occasionally heard of friends, or friends of friends, who weren't "finding their place" here. I suspected that boredom was the cause. Baruch Hashem, I'm not bored, I would think. I didn't know what I would do without my job. Besides the income, I needed the full schedule.

Tishah B'Av night, Gavriel and I walked to the Mir to hear Eichah. I found a spot on the floor of the crowded women's section. Some women had brought low stools. I wish I had thought of that.

Suddenly, I looked up and saw Gavriel standing in the doorway, a low stool in his hands. I smiled. He thought of me. He wants me to be comfortable. Maybe it's because I'm pregnant? Thank you, Gavriel.

I settled down again on the stool and looked around. Who were these other women gathered here tonight? Some were young girls, with braids hanging down their backs. Some looked older, chashuv. Who knows who they could be? They could have been well-known rebbetzins, and I, the ignorant American, would have no idea.

Even though I live here now, I still feel like a tourist. I wondered if that feeling would ever go away. Will I always feel out of place?

A hush came over the assemblage, and the ancient words of Eichah came through the latticework mechitzah, pouring into our hearts. Some of the older women cried. This is why we came, I thought. To hear Eichah in Yerushalayim.

Shanah Rishonah in Jerusalem
— Shaina Hoffman*

Living in Jerusalem had always been my dream. I didn't anticipate doing so for good, but a few years sure sounded like the ideal plan. And so, when I was going out with Ari and he mentioned his dream of starting off married life in Israel, I was thrilled.

Five months later, we found ourselves in a little apartment in the heart of Jerusalem. The place was small, cramped, and a little dilapidated, but my heart was bursting with positive energy. I looked forward to building my little home into a warm and loving one together with my husband. I enjoyed the challenge of trying to cook with different ingredients, and I loved to joke about the mistakes I made along the way. Jerusalem was teeming with life and sunshine, and that perfectly blended into the picture of my life. Life simply couldn't be better; we were flying high. And then, as if all the stars shone at once, we received the news: we were expecting a baby.

I remember sitting with my husband on the balcony, enjoying the Israeli summer evening breeze, smiles crossing our faces as we discussed our promising future. My husband's joy was written all over his face, and his gait even took on a more positive rhythm. We shared the news with our parents from the other side of the ocean, and they shed tears of joy and wished us the very best. I remember putting down the phone and feeling a twinge in my heart; we were so far away.

The next few weeks passed in a blissful blur. I was feeling great and worked hard stocking up my freezer, being sure the day would come when I would be too nauseous to step into the kitchen.

That day never came.

The day it happened will be indelibly engraved in my heart. It was as if all the positive exciting hues that continually danced before me waved good-bye, and all that was left for my eyes to see was red. We ran to the doctor, in the hope of being saved from our most dreaded nightmare, but hope was not forthcoming when the doctor so softly and gently informed us we had lost the baby.

It was too harsh of a reality to actually be a reality and too painful for pain. The doctor patted me on my shoulder. "It's early, very typical of a first pregnancy, and happens to a third of young women."

These words did not manage to comfort me. I was shattered. We were both shattered. Our world had just been crushed.

As we stood in the elevator, we gave each other encouraging eye contact but couldn't talk. I took my cell phone out of my pocket and glared grimly at what was to be my due date. It stared back at me in a mocking way. I began to erase it. It took me a while to delete the exclamation marks and smiles that surrounded it. I remember happily adding them every time I would glance at that date. Now it would be void of any meaning.

Walking alongside my husband, I remember telling him how I felt this nisayon was so much easier to handle with him at my side. It was as if we were each holding the handle of a heavy suitcase, struggling to carry it together.

It was then that I realized my husband's strength. When we got home that evening, I cried like never before. My husband was there with me, encouraging and strengthening me. His words were as soft as butter that oiled my cracking heart. We spoke for hours. We both revealed our innermost feelings and tried hard to comfort each other.

They say marriage is like a candle: it grows brighter when the hour gets darker. As we sat together on the porch talking until the darkest moments of the night, it was then that I sensed its true meaning.

The next few days that followed were difficult ones. We found ourselves in the hospital most of the time dealing with all the technicalities that came attached to our miscarriage. At this time, we truly felt the distance from our parents, who might have helped us with our physical and emotional needs had they lived closer. My husband really extended himself, ensuring we had an adequate amount of food and drinks all the time. He constantly stood at my bedside and dealt with the doctors and all the necessary technical arrangements. I marveled at his competence and the immense strength he displayed. His care and devotion were the greatest comfort and a most wonderful builder of our relationship. It tied the two of us into a tighter knot of respect and admiration.

A few months later, shopping in Geulah with my husband, I mentioned how much I realize that living in Israel I had only one person to depend on. What more could one ask for than a dedicated husband to be that one person when traveling through shanah rishonah?

I gazed around at the couples passing us on the streets; many looked dazed and overwhelmed. I wanted to stop and tell them how wonderful Jerusalem was for their shalom bayis. I so much wished I could explain to them how much they should appreciate the benefit of being here together with no one else, just the two of them.

At our next visit to the Kosel, I fingered the wall with a heart full of emotion. I literally felt Hashem standing right beside me, stroking my cheeks. My eyes were brimming with tears as I opened my Tehillim and thanked Hashem for the nisayon that He had so lovingly handed to me. I expressed my appreciation that the nisayon was one where I immediately saw its benefits. I was grateful that after such emotional turmoil, I was able to come here and feel Hashem's presence so close to my heart.

The beige wall blurred before me as I gazed up toward the brilliant blue sky. I felt Hashem wrap His arms around me, and my heart blazed with strong emotion for the moment I was presently living through. I felt so close to my Father, and I was so grateful to be living in His home.

Chapter 7

An Extra Blessing in Shanah Rishonah: When You're Expecting in the First Year

As we dreamed about our wedding days for years, we also dreamed about the day we would become mothers. If you are expecting in *shanah rishonah*, there is a chance you are elated, shocked, maybe a little scared, and, hopefully, beside yourself with joy.

There is also a chance you are sicker than you knew you could be, wondering what happened to the you of just a few weeks or months ago, the one who made delicious dinners, loved going out and spending time with your new husband, and generally felt good all the time.

For many women, the gift of expecting in *shanah rishonah* can be both wonderful and overwhelming. There are sure to be a lot of adjustments, and the year is certain to be exciting and full of things that you have never experienced before.

When you are expecting a baby during *shanah rishonah,* the reality and often pressure of having a baby is on your mind. In life many things are not about their simple realities, but about how you look at them and deal with them. Do you let your situation inspire you or discourage you? Do you place your faith in Hashem or do you let insecurities guide your reactions? Recognizing your feelings, whatever they are — excitement, joy, or confusion — can be the start of getting through this aspect of *shanah rishonah* happily.

If you are expecting, mazel tov. May this be a year of health and joy for you, your husband, and your baby. Everything is about to change; with Hashem's help, it will be for the better.

The first moments you hold your baby in your arms are indescribably powerful, the year that follows more magical and, likely, more exhausting than you can imagine. There is a moment when you look into your baby's eyes, feel his or her skin against yours, and realize that this child has been entrusted to you from the Al-mighty. You have been given the most precious gift in the world, and now you have a mission to raise the best child you possibly can, to be the best mother and wife you can be with this new set of challenges and gifts in front of you, and to raise this child to Torah, *chuppah,* and *ma'asim tovim.*

What to Expect When You're Expecting in the First Year

———————————————————————————• *Chana Herzog*

I think it's the question that's at the back of every young couple's minds when they enter their first year of marriage. What on earth will happen if we're expecting right away? Will we still be able to have a good time together? Is it the end of our blissful "honeymoon"? Will we have time for each other anymore? Will everything change?

I hate to be the one to say it, but for us, yes, things changed. Once I was expecting, if we went to an amusement park together, we weren't exactly waving our hands in the air on an upside-down roller coaster like we had in the past. Now we were slowly strolling through the park, water bottle in hand, and stopping at every available bench for a rest. When we went out to eat, I would spend most of the evening studying the menu trying to find something to order that didn't make me want to gag. And if my husband thought it took me a while to get ready to go out before, when I was expecting I would try on my entire wardrobe twice before I found something remotely flattering to wear.

Now, when I look back at that time in my life, one recurring image comes to mind: me throwing up and my husband cleaning up.

It was only about three months into our marriage and a few weeks of expecting when I started to learn what affection is really all about. There I was, not exactly resembling the girl my husband had dated. Instead I was pale, tired, emotional, and throwing up. Not a very attractive state. And there he was, kneeling down beside me with a look of genuine concern and sympathy on his face, gently asking me what he could do to make me feel better.

Call me crazy, but as terrible as that sounds, that was one of the most special times we had shared together. Yes, we have shared many candlelit dinners; we've walked through the gardens of New York's Central Park in the spring; we've sailed the waters of Venice in a private gondola. We loved those times, but I think that, honestly, anyone would. But how ironic that at the point when I was feeling my worst was the time that brought out the best in us as a couple and made us so much closer.

I guess it's because when it comes down to it, you can't just be in a marriage for the fun of it. Many a couple has been on perfect dates, and many a couple has broken up soon after. The difference is, in a committed marriage, you're not just there for the candlelit dinners; you're in it to build a family.

Since our son came into the world, I feel more connected to my husband than I ever did before. I think it's because we now need each other on a whole new level. Not only do I need him to carry the stroller up the stairs for me, but I also need his companionship and support in keeping it all together. And I think he needs mine, too.

Listen, life isn't always all rosy, and neither is any normal relationship. Since we became parents there definitely are some extra things to argue about.

"You change his diaper."

"No, you change his diaper."

"I'm so tired!"

"So am I!"

I'm sure you get the picture... But nothing breaks up an argument better than a squeal of laughter from your baby right in the heat of it. Your heart could literally just melt, and seriously, nothing else matters.

There is a recurring image that comes to mind when I think about the birth of our baby. One night, at about 3 in the morning, I had nursed my baby, but he refused to go back to sleep. Too tired to deal with it, I passed him on to my husband. I turned over and tried to get some sleep. From the corner of my eye, I saw the most adorable thing in the world. My little baby and his father lying arm in arm, playing with each other's hands, looking at each other and smiling.

That's what it's all about, the not feeling good, the emotional ups and downs, and the new relationship you and your husband have to build now around a third person. It is moments like those that make it all worthwhile.

Whatever You Do, Do It With Simchah
● Ilana Solomon

When I first brought my husband-to-be home to meet my parents, I told him that he must shake my father's hand and call my parents Mr. and Mrs. Kanoff. In turn, he told me that I shouldn't dare call his parents Mr. and Mrs. Solomon. They were used to being called by their first names and preferred it that way. It didn't take long to see that if we were going to be together, we were going to have to merge two very different worlds.

I remember my father's amused expression as he spoke to my future husband, Mayer, for the first time after we were engaged. "So you're a musician. How exactly do you plan on supporting my daughter and a family? You didn't go to college, did you?"

Although my parents liked him very much, they were parents, and he didn't have a good enough answer to any of my father's questions.

Planning the wedding was a riot. I wanted a fancy, Cinderellalike wedding, and my husband didn't understand why we couldn't just get married in Israel on his parents' moshav. He even told me that he would plant grass in the soccer field a few months in advance so that the ground would be green by the time we got married. As sweet an offer as that was, I declined. I wanted place cards and sushi. He wanted to know if he had to wear a tie.

Until we actually made it to the chuppah, I was still sure that I was dreaming. I'm not funny enough for him, cool enough, smart enough... But there we were blissfully standing under the chuppah. We had made it. We were married.

An Extra Blessing in Shanah Rishonah: | 149

A few weeks later we found out we were expecting. Needless to say, we were overjoyed the moment we found out. Every selfish fear I'd had about having children disappeared right away.

Things started to change, and I thought the things that were happening to me were normal pregnancy things. I was exhausted, my joints were hurting me, and my skin was pale with a yellow tint. None of it seemed red-flag worthy. Even when one of my fifth-grade students told me that my nose looked funny (I didn't notice, but my cartilage was collapsing and my nose was caving in), I didn't ask my doctor any questions.

Finally, my midwife sent me to get my blood work done after one of our visits because she didn't like the way I looked. As I left the office, I saw that on my folder she had put a red sticker saying "high risk."

I drove over to my family doctor to have my blood taken and waited in a private room for fifteen minutes until they got the results. The knot in my stomach was getting bigger by the moment. I had no idea what was going on. When the doctor came back in, she told me that the blood results showed that my kidneys were working at 15 percent and I should get myself over to the emergency room right away.

"Should I get in an ambulance or can my husband drive me? Do you mind if I call my parents? What exactly does this mean?"

All the questions came out together, but she could only answer the first two. "You can have your husband drive you and, yes, you can call your parents, but I don't really know what is happening to you."

It was one of the nights of Chanukah, and my husband was playing a concert at the local shul. I called him right away to tell him what was going on.

I drove from the doctor to pick him up, and then we switched seats. My parents met us at the hospital, visibly worried. They waited in the waiting room patiently for hours until there was any news to tell them. The baby was fine, but they were running tests to see the cause of my potential kidney failure.

Once I was admitted and in a bed in a private room, my husband called every friend we had to divide up the book of Tehillim. Within an hour, we had given out the whole book, and people were pledging to take it on for as long as we needed. People whose siddurim were on the shelves collecting dust pledged to take on Tehillim as a merit for my refuah.

After five days of being questioned by every doctor and medical student in the hospital's rheumatology department, they found that I had an autoimmune disease called Wegener's granulomatosis. The nose caving in was very common among people with this disease; it even had a name: "saddle nose."

Wegener's is an inflammatory disease, and it can affect the upper respiratory system, the lungs, and the kidneys. With me, it had already attacked my sinuses and kidneys. They immediately put me on a very high dose of steroids and were researching what other medication could be used during pregnancy.

The options they presented to us were horrible and worse than horrible. We had two choices. The first option was to take an extremely strong drug that had a good chance of putting this disease into remission, but since it was so toxic, it would endanger the baby. There was also a 40 percent chance that I would no longer be able to have children after using this medication.

The second option was to take a drug that was not a danger to the baby, but because it was weaker, it might not work. So our options were to either lose the baby or possibly my own life.

I cannot even imagine the feelings my husband was experiencing during those first days after they diagnosed my disease. I felt horrible that he thought he had married a healthy woman who was going to bear his children and raise a family, and here I was in a hospital bed and we were making life-or-death decisions five months after our wedding.

My husband was amazing. He sat by my bed, listened to the doctors, asked a million questions, and davened. It was during this time that I came to the realization that he was truly my soul mate and that he was going to stand by me through anything. We were in this together, and he was not going to bail out, ever.

We were given two weeks to decide which drug to take. We agreed we needed to consult with a rav about whether I should take the stronger drug, even though the doctors had advised against it as it would probably deform the fetus significantly, or take the less effective drug that most likely wouldn't work. We were set to meet the Skverer Rebbe, a tzaddik who was known to be very knowledgeable in the field of medicine.

We drove into New Square in our sports car, and I asked a young man, probably about fifteen, for directions to get to the Rebbe. He just stared at me and then looked at my husband. My husband asked him how to get to the Rebbe, and he gave him directions. I had never felt so out of place my whole life. I was from Queens, having grown up in a Modern Orthodox community, and this was a different world. One would think growing up in an Orthodox community that I would have known to let my husband do the talking, but I was clueless.

When we finally got in to see the Rebbe, I sat stiffly and made sure not to say a word while my husband explained the whole situation to him. Then the Rebbe turned to me and asked, "Do you have anything to add?"

It was like looking into the face of an angel. I was speechless, so I shook my head no, and listened to his advice. He told us to seek the advice of a specific doctor who was an expert in this field and to follow whatever advice he gave us. Then he added, "Whatever you do, do it with simchah. It will be all right."

The next day we called the specialist's office, but it just so happened that he was on vacation in Europe that week. We asked anyone and everyone if they knew how to get in touch with the doctor because our time was running out.

Miraculously, within twenty-four hours we received a phone call from Europe. It was the doctor saying that he heard we were looking for him.

Evidently the game of Jewish geography had worked, and we had a free telephone consultation with one of the top rheumatologists in the world. He advised us to take the less dangerous drug, wished us luck, and said that he would like to meet with us when he returned from vacation for a free face-to-face consultation. We were overjoyed. We finally had a direction to take — and we were going to do it with simchah.

When we informed the doctors of our decision, they said that they would wait to do a C-section until the baby was developed enough, and then they would switch me over to the stronger medication. I didn't outwardly argue, but I knew that I would never agree to take a medication that left me with such a high chance of being unable to have more children.

I began the medication, and the next phase of my healing began. I had to quit my job as a teacher because my *immune system was seriously compromised and I couldn't be around anyone who was sick. While I spent much of my time at doctors' offices, my husband was spending more and more time learning, something he hadn't done much of since his childhood. He began to stay in shul after the morning minyan to learn a bit more. He would come home at around 11 a.m., and then he would take me to all of my appointments or he would work.*

As I regained my strength and was able to be more independent, 11 o'clock became noon and then 1, when he got hungry and had to come home for lunch. His baseball cap was switched for a kippah, and he began speaking of learning in a proper yeshivah for half a day.

I was also beginning on a road of personal growth that had been stagnant for quite a while. Seeing my body react positively to the medication and knowing that the baby was healthy made me realize how grateful I was to just be alive, and I didn't want to waste a moment of my precious life. I began saying Tehillim every day and listening to shiurim in the car instead of music on the radio.

Together, we were beginning a journey that G-d knew we were destined to find, that up until that point we had stayed away from and now were ready to take. The greatest feeling was that we were doing it together.

At one of my doctor appointments, I saw an obviously religious Jewish woman holding her newborn son. I started up a conversation with her and commented how adorable her baby was and asked her his name. She replied, "Abraham." I asked her if that's what they called him, and she said they called him Avrumi. I realized that this woman had no idea I was Jewish. Even though I had a scarf on my head, my jeans and sweatshirt didn't exactly scream "religious Jewish woman."

I was so broken. Even though I was growing and changing so much on the inside, my outside looked the same as ever. I decided that I wanted to have my outside match my inside. I was more than happy to go on a shopping spree and bought lots of new stylish skirts and longer-sleeved shirts.

My husband and I were each becoming more committed to a Torah way of life in our own way, but standing side by side doing it. My husband has an intense personality, and when he does something, he does it 100 percent. I felt like I was riding on his coattails, but luckily we were going in the same direction.

The weeks went by and my kidney function was slowly increasing and the baby was growing steadily. The pregnancy progressed week after week. The baby was doing fine and so was I. So they held off on the C-section.

They scheduled a C-section for a point that they felt the baby had developed enough, which was chol hamo'ed Pesach, saying that by then the baby was full term and there would be no negative effects of bringing him into the world four weeks early. The doctors were amazed that we had come so far and did not want to take any additional risks by letting the pregnancy progress further.

At thirty-five weeks and five days, I went into labor. It was Shabbos and Pesach, and we were far from the hospital. We drove to the hospital and when we arrived, we literally jumped out of the car. The parking attendant asked my husband if he could move the car up a bit. "Sorry, it's Shabbos!" he yelled and off we ran.

We ate our first Pesach seder together in my hospital room. Twelve hours later, a 3 pound 11 ounce baby boy was born and, baruch Hashem, he was perfect. Three weeks later, he was named Rafael Moshe Nes, and we were the proud, thankful, overjoyed parents of a new little neshamah.

The road ahead of us was still long and painful, but the hardest part was over. Rafael was what we were waiting for. I never switched over to the other medication, and now, almost ten years later, we are living happily with three little boys. I am still battling my disease, but now with a much lighter medication, strict diet, and natural therapies. My husband is living his new dream of learning Torah full-time.

I think back a few years and remember my husband asking me if he could grow a beard. I said no. Now he has a full beard. Then he asked me if he could grow out his peyos. I said no. Now they're too long to keep behind his ears. By the time he asked me if he could wear a long black jacket, I gave up. I realized that becoming a family meant that anything one of us did that brought us closer to Hashem, as external as it seemed, was really good for the growth of all of us.

The Magnanimous Task Called Motherhood

● Esther Gross*

When I was a child, I never really appreciated all the fine details that made my home run as smoothly and efficiently as it did. In my limited viewpoint, all my needs were simply taken care of. My clothes could always be found freshly laundered and folded in their particular drawer. There was plenty of food in the fridge no matter when I opened the door to forage for something to eat. Cookies were always waiting for me with a glass of milk when I came home from school, and somehow all my outfits were coordinated with those of my siblings on Shabbos and yom tov.

These were a few of the many things that I took for granted. I never stopped to think just how organized and efficient my mother had to be to get these fine little elements together. This was the reality of my world, and I was completely satisfied in accepting it as fact.

I guess it wasn't until I got married and started being in charge of all these countless domestic tasks and details that I began to truly appreciate my mother. I always loved and admired her abilities, but somehow, when these tasks become solely a girl's responsibility, she realizes just how intricate they really are. How did my mother manage everything on her own? I could not imagine being able to do everything that she was capable of.

After I got married, I thought that I would have time to learn everything I needed to know about keeping a house: cooking, cleaning, shopping, laundry, budgeting, paying bills. Wasn't that what shanah rishonah was for? Wasn't it a year to get used to all these adjustments, especially the most important one of getting to know my new husband?

One thing I hadn't counted on was finding out I was expecting after only six weeks of marriage.

After being married for less than a couple of months, my husband had to deal with seeing me suffer through morning sickness. I wanted to look my best and impress him with all my fine accomplishments, but I felt as though the energy had been zapped out of me. Laundry, cooking, and other household chores were put on the back burner while I needed extended time to sleep.

When I finally felt like I had learned to fit working, shopping, cooking, and cleaning into my daily schedule, the magnanimous job of motherhood was thrust upon me. I loved my new daughter to pieces. From the moment she was born, I knew that my life would become even more fulfilling with her a part of it. Yet no one could have pre-

pared me for the twenty-four-hour job that this new par-
enting role entailed.

Between feedings, changing diapers, analyzing every cry
to decipher what exactly each one meant, I realized that
my mother was even more of a superwoman than I had
originally thought. How could I ever be able to maintain
her standards of running a house when I was barely man-
aging to get enough sleep between feedings so I wouldn't
collapse from fatigue? A gourmet meal to me became one
where not a single item was warmed up in the microwave.

It finally dawned on me what an enormous task this
motherhood undertaking really was. My new baby relied
solely on me for her sustenance and comfort. She was com-
pletely dependent on me and would not offer one compli-
ment or thank-you in return to keep me going. When you
first get married and you prepare a delicious meal for your
husband, a thank-you is the least you expect from him to
acknowledge all your efforts on his behalf. Yet parenthood
is not like marriage at all.

Hashem in His infinite wisdom has given us two
incredible means to deal with parenthood. He has estab-
lished within each baby an endearing cuteness and utter
adorable quality, which attaches the parents to the child
from the moment he is born. He also implanted within
the parents a natural, constant feeling of unconditional
love toward their new baby.

As I look down at my beautiful little bundle, I realize
that motherhood is an incredible gift and worth every glo-
rious minute. I am certain my mother went through the
same adjustments and insecurities, but baruch Hashem
she lived through them and managed. I am not sure when
I can see myself doing everything that she was able to do,
yet there is strength and encouragement in knowing what
she was able to accomplish.

My husband and I learned in shanah rishonah to deal with things as they come up. Our bond has strengthened in our greatest achievement yet: that of becoming parents. Sleep is a thing of the past, and meals are, more often than I would like to admit, pretty basic.

I also have a different focus than when I first got married. Now, instead of learning how to juggle all of my responsibilities as well as my mother did, I focus on my daughter's precious new achievements, like a crooked little smile, a wave bye-bye, a new word, a tiny first step. It is her achievements and my being here to witness them that give me the strength to make it through each and every day.

Expecting in Shanah Rishonah

● Beth Shapiro

"Oh, I always loved being pregnant," said my friend, who was in her forties, wistfully. "That feeling — it's indescribable." And her face glowed as she remembered what it was like to be pregnant.

I've had this conversation many times with different people. Some of them older, some of them younger, and I've never understood it. That is not what it's like for me to be pregnant — not at all.

I found out I was expecting my first child three months after Simcha and I were married. We got the news and were ecstatic — for three days. Then I woke up one morning nauseous, barely able to lift my head from the pillow. I fell back into bed, unable to get up. That is, until this horrible retching feeling overcame me, and I ran out of the room to throw up. Then, shocked, I crawled back in bed. And that is where I basically stayed for the next three months.

It was late spring in Israel and it was hot, so I would lie in bed, drenched in perspiration and moaning, from the moment Simcha left in the morning until the moment he came home in the evening.

There was this smell. It was such a terrible smell. And it emanated from some unknown location in the kitchen. It tortured me. And I couldn't find the source of it.

"Do you smell it?" I asked Simcha. "I can't take it." But he couldn't smell it.

One morning, after he left for yeshivah, I crawled out of bed determined to find the smell and defeat it. I needed to take back my life. I girded my strength. I cleaned counters, I moved furniture, I scrubbed the floor on my hands and knees — all the time sniffing and searching. But in the end, the smell remained, and only I, in my pregnant state, could smell it.

We lived in a beautiful apartment that year at the bottom of a very large hill. The closest supermarket was a twenty-minute walk completely uphill.

I called my husband one day at yeshivah. He had no cell phone, so I had to call the pay phone in the hallway and ask someone to take him out of seder. "Simcha, I'm so sorry to do this. I need you."

"Are you O.K.?" he asked, clearly worried at being called out of seder.

"No," I moaned. "I'm not O.K.. I can't eat, and I'm so hungry. I don't know what to do."

"Beth," he answered uncertainly, "what can I do? I'm at yeshivah."

I have to interrupt this story to relate two important facts. Fact one is that I am not an intrinsically needy person. I had lived on my own for more than ten years before I got married. I had a responsible job, supported myself, and took good care of myself.

The second is that Simcha, at the time, was a fourth-year medical student. He had taken a year off from his studies to learn in yeshivah, but he was almost a doctor. And he was a compassionate doctor with a gentle, caring bedside manner. He knew how to empathize with people, and he knew how to help people.

"I don't know," I said weakly. "Can you please just come home? I can't be alone."

There was a pause. "You want me to come home?"

"Yes," I whimpered. "And please go to the store and bring me some of that Ensure stuff from the supermarket."

"The dietary supplement?" he asked incredulously. "You want a dietary supplement?"

"Yes, I need some nutrition. I think I'm dying." There was silence. "Please —" I begged. "I'm so sorry."

And so he came home and brought me the supplement. I lifted my sweaty head from the bed and sipped the chocolaty shake. Then I promptly threw up.

I continued like this for months. I sent him for spaghetti one night, which I ended up finding disgusting. The thought of salmon made me retch. He suggested a homeopathic remedy, and I shouted at him. It was not a simple time. The doctor didn't think there was anything particularly wrong with me. "You're pregnant," he said. "It's like that for some women."

The doctor was right. It is like that for some women when they are expecting. My situation was by no means the worst, but I definitely do not glow when I am pregnant.

But although during my four subsequent pregnancies I have never felt well, I have never felt as bad as I did the first time. There are a few things that I wish I had known — things that would have made it easier for me.

Today I pass these gems along:

1. *It only lasts nine months. When I was flat on my back, feeling ill and depleted, I was certain that this was my new reality and I would feel like this forever. Those nine months felt like forever. But I felt good again and you will, too. That food you used to love that makes you sick — you will love it again.*

2. *There is a minhag in some communities not to tell people that you are expecting during the first three months of pregnancy. I understand why this minhag exists. People are nervous about ayin hara. But what I've learned is that people who are often around pregnant women can tell when a person is expecting and struggling. You think they don't know. But they do. So tell them and ask for help. Often, they want to help but are respecting your privacy. By asking for help, you give them a chance to give it to you and get a chance to learn from their experience.*

3. *If you live in a yeshivah community, far from home, with lots of other young newlyweds, tell someone else. I know you have no energy, but find a mentor. If you can't get out of bed, ask your husband to find you a mentor. You need to know that you are normal, and you need impartial help. It is too much for a brand-new husband to shoulder the responsibility of a nonfunctioning wife.*

4. *When you pick a mentor, pick one, not seven. Don't ask seven people for advice or you will spend your little bit of energy trying to sort through everyone's advice and will make yourself crazy.*

5. *Don't let your stomach get empty. I'd heard this, but I really wish I had listened. I would wake up with an empty stomach and dry-heave. If I had heeded the advice to keep food in my stomach, I still would have been sick, but never that sick.*

6. *Try to identify your triggers. One thing I learned is that I feel dreadfully hot when I am pregnant. I actually feel about ten degrees hotter than the rest of the world, which makes summertime the worst. I have learned to compensate for this by constantly eating ice pops, drinking cold drinks, and putting cold compresses on my neck.*

7. *Remember that even though you feel sick, your pregnancy is also really hard on your husband. He feels helpless and clueless and abandoned. If you can't do anything about that, at least recognize it and tell him you know. If you have the strength, try to give him some special attention.*

8. *Give your life some structure. One of the biggest problems I had during my first pregnancy was a lack of structure. I was learning, but it wasn't mandatory. With my subsequent children, I learned that forcing myself out of bed and out of the house gave me periods of the day when I could feel like I was accomplishing things. That made me stronger.*

As I write this more than twelve years later, I still feel the pain of many of the experiences I went through when I was pregnant for the first time. But it is more like reading a terrible story that happened to someone else. Today, I have a beautiful bas mitzvah girl and twelve years of memories with her: first steps, first words, siddur parties, Pesach cleaning. And while the beginning was rough, looking back, I wouldn't trade a moment of it.

Chapter 8

When You Aren't Expecting in Shanah Rishonah

With all of the preparations for the wedding, an average *kallah* will wonder about many things. What will life be like after the *chuppah*? Where will we live? What will it be like to be a wife? Will he like my cooking? Will I like his mother? Will she like me?

Another common question in many women's minds is that of having children. Will they come right away, or will we enjoy months of quiet dinners and Shabbos-afternoon walks?

Many women never question whether they will find themselves expecting, only how soon. But as we know, Hashem has His individual plans for all of us, and for some women the first year of marriage will come and go without a sign that a baby is coming. Many of these women are destined to have children, *b'ezras Hashem*, but not necessarily in the time they thought they would. For some women, having to wait even a little will drive them to the doctors with questions like "What is wrong with us? When will it happen? And what is taking so long?"

Shanah rishonah can be filled with both tremendous joy and, sometimes, a nagging longing and even pain. For those who aren't yet expecting a new addition as the year progresses, the intensity can grow. The question of will it happen at all can rear its ugly head, supported by many who don't realize it is insensitive to make jokes or ask inquisitively, "Anything you want to tell me?"

I can share of my own experience that it wasn't the waiting as much as the comments of well-meaning friends, neighbors, and family members that caused unnecessary pain and lots of self-doubt to creep into my first year and eventually taint it.

If you are waiting anxiously for the day you receive a positive test result, *b'ezras Hashem,* we should hear good news in the right time. In the meantime, trust in Hashem, just as you have in every aspect of your life thus far.

When babies come, they are a wonderful blessing, but for now, enjoy the blessing Hashem has given you. You have time alone with your husband to get to know each other and enjoy all those nights you get to sleep straight through. *B'ezras Hashem,* this quiet time won't last forever, and once it is gone, with Hashem's help you won't ever have this much sleep or quiet again.

It's Not Even a Year Yet

● *Tehilla Shapiro**

At first I was too busy adjusting to married life and learning how to run a house to think about pregnancy. But as the months passed, I did wonder. And worry.

Why should I be worried? I asked myself. Lots of people don't have babies right away. Look at this friend and that one — And now they have one, two, three children pulling at their skirts whenever they try to go anywhere. Enjoy the peace and quiet while it lasts.

My own mother, who eventually had nine children, also didn't have a baby right away. As the oldest of the brood, I grew up hearing the story of her two-and-a-half-year wait, of the tactless woman who approached my parents at a wedding several years after their marriage and said, "You know, you should really see a doctor." My mother smiled and told her, "Thanks for the advice, but I'm already expecting."

So I had never thought babies had to come right away. In my mind, babies came after you'd settled into your new reality and gotten accustomed to this new relationship called marriage. But somehow, actually being faced with the specter of childlessness was something completely different.

It's not even a year yet, I told myself again and again. The mantra didn't hold water. My maternal instinct had somehow been aroused in a way it hadn't been when I was single, and I wanted to know that feeling of expectancy that my friends did.

Finally, our first anniversary nearly upon us, my worried husband consulted with his rosh yeshivah, who directed us to a frum fertility expert in our city.

"It happens to lots of newly married couples." The doctor, sporting a trim gray beard and a warm smile, set us at ease immediately. "I want you to make an appointment with Doctor Cohn."

The specialist, Dr. Cohn, who had gone through this experience herself, had one wall in her office devoted to pictures of her hard-won blond little girl. She cheerfully outlined a course of treatment, assuring me that my problems could be taken care of easily, with Hashem's help.

Within three months, I was expecting. My gorgeous little boy was born a month shy of our second anniversary, and a second followed quickly on his heels.

Today, looking back, I often think how lucky I was that I had that extra time to settle in, to adjust to marriage before I had to think about babies. Seeing the other side of the coin, friends and relatives who spend three-quarters of shanah rishonah feeling sick and exhausted and trying to build a relationship at the same time, I'm glad I had it the other way.

But I haven't forgotten that twinge of pain, of fear, that I experienced in those months of waiting. It's a twinge that helps me empathize with other people who are going through the same thing, wondering, worrying, thinking, When will my time come?

If I'd Known It Was Going to Happen Eventually!

•— Zippy Cohen*

At first, I was all right with it. I enjoyed the first few months of my married life. There was so much going on: settling into living with someone else, creating a home from four white square walls, figuring out how to make dinner, and more. I was so overwhelmed with the reality of my new life, in a new country, with a new husband, that not having a baby on the way wasn't a huge concern.

But then the comments started. At a birthday party for one of my new nieces, someone asked if I wanted a slice of pizza. I responded that I was fleishig. Then I heard, "She's probably not up to eating. I never want to eat in the beginning." I couldn't believe my ears. What chutzpah! If I was expecting, I would have been embarrassed, but I wasn't expecting, so I was just sad and hurt.

A few more months passed and still no news. I went to the doctor, who told me that it was too soon to worry. Seven months isn't enough time to get nervous; I should only start feeling concern after a year with no positive results.

As the year ended, I went back to the doctor. He ran a few tests. An ultrasound showed I had thirty gallstones, each the size of a pinky nail. The doctor looked at me, relieved that I wasn't expecting. He told me that my condition would have made pregnancy incredibly dangerous, and I was lucky I wasn't expecting before taking care of this. The next step was to schedule an operation to have my gallbladder removed.

Being totally terrified of surgery, I asked if I could try to get rid of them on my own. He said for now that it would be all right.

Eight months of acupuncture and other types of alternative medicine later, I was so sick I couldn't sleep through an entire night without getting up to retch.

I'm a private person and didn't feel I had to share my health issues with the world or the rest of the family. Only my husband and my mother knew what I was going through and how sick I was. And thus the comments and jokes didn't stop. When I chatted on the phone with friends from New York or California, they always managed to drop into the conversation a line here or there like "So, anything you want to tell me?" One even asked flatly, "Are you expecting yet?"

I didn't want to go into my health condition, and yet I felt embarrassed by the question. It seemed to me that people expected something from me, and by not having news to offer, I was failing them.

Eventually I got good at dodging the comments. But one particularly oversensitive day, someone came up to me on the street. I had made the mistake of wearing an oversize dress to let my tender middle breathe after a night of being sick again. She was a woman I had met once at my aunt's house. She came up to me and said, "So I see there is a b'sha'ah tovah in order."

I lost it. I completely snapped. I didn't say it in a rude tone, but I looked her in the eye and said, "You aren't allowed to ask questions that can embarrass a person. When there is something to talk about, I'll let you know."

Unfortunately, I embarrassed her in the process and certainly didn't feel very good about myself by the end of the exchange. I realized that my life was too difficult this way. More than I was afraid of having surgery, I was afraid of never being able to have and take care of a baby if I didn't get this handled. I know it sounds funny, but I missed the neshamah that I felt was waiting to come to us.

I scheduled the surgery, and, by a miracle, a top surgeon who knew my husband's family and had trained at a top medical center had an opening a mere eleven days later. Normally, you had to schedule him months in advance and pay thousands of dollars privately.

People say you can't explain the pains of birth unless you lived through it, but I would choose birth any day after what I experienced recovering from that surgery. The surgery was fine, but the recovery that was supposed to take three to four days took me six to eight weeks in bed, in more pain than I knew how to deal with. I couldn't fathom how people could say it took only one month to recover fully from this type of surgery. The recovery was so painful. I felt half-dead, and a month had already passed.

My husband was the supportive, loving prince that a woman, in time of need, dreams about. I saw in those weeks how he took care of me and knew that when we had children, they would have the world's most loving, gentle father.

Baruch Hashem, I recovered. Within nine weeks, I was back to myself. Seven months after the surgery, while walking to the Kosel on Shabbos, I had a strong intuition. I realized that at that very moment, I could be pregnant.

Shortly after, I found out that, *b'ezras Hashem*, we would be parents. Though I'd been anxiously awaiting the news from right after I'd recovered from surgery, Hashem gave us that extra time. In reality, I needed it to fully recover both physically and emotionally.

If I had known in the beginning it was going to happen eventually, I would have saved myself much heartache and unnecessary worry. Truth be told, our baby came at the exact right moment for us as a couple. When I look back, any sooner wouldn't have been better. Thank You, Hashem, for knowing what we needed so much more clearly than we did.

Challenges Along the Way

●Esther Miller*

Life takes us to unexpected crossroads and journeys, which we never envisioned when standing underneath the chuppah. I can recall becoming engaged at twenty-one, thinking that this would be the beginning of a beautiful life. I didn't exactly know where life was taking me, but I had a few pieces in place. As I walked down to the chuppah on a white runner lined with lavender, pink, and white rose petals, I knew one thing for certain: this was the onset of an incredible life with my husband, my bashert. This would be a life where I would become a mother to children and begin to build my bayis ne'eman b'Yisrael.

Soon we learn that life progresses on its way and things don't always turn out the way we imagined they would. Hashem controls the world, and He often shows us His connection to us through our day-to-day experiences. Many times in our lives we are taken down a path that we would not normally choose for ourselves. A path that is filled with many points where we can grow, strive, and become even better ovdei Hashem. Yet we don't always see this aspect of things. It's sometimes very hard to believe that this pre-ordained path is truly ours. Did Hashem really have me in mind for this nisayon, this particular test? This really does not seem fitting for me, we keep telling ourselves. There must have been some sort of mistake.

Looking back at everything that transpired, I realize that I took things for granted. It's pretty hard not to, though, in our circles, when everyone around us seems to be blessed with many children. Everything is geared around family, which is how it should be. Yet I realize now, in hindsight, that this enables us to become disconnected with each living miracle that we are zocheh to witness.

People say that if Hashem would just show them an open miracle, then they would for sure be able to recognize His greatness and serve Him with a complete heart no matter what their religious affiliation. However, unfortunately, we have become blinded. We fail to see the miracle of each birth. We see families with, kenaina hara, eight, nine, ten children, so we just assume that this is the norm. Therefore I, like many of us, never gave childbirth much thought. I just assumed that after you get married you have children: the next step to building your bayis. Isn't this what every woman was created to do? Why should I be any different?

How wrong I was.

After you marry, everyone around you seems to be wondering the same thing: Is she pregnant? There are even people who will ask you directly. I still remember going to my friend's shower after a few months of marriage. I am not too sure what prompted the interchange; I guess maybe I had put on a few pounds after the wedding. Out of all the people to ask me, it was the mother of the kallah. She said, in front of everyone, "So, when are you due?" I remember feeling very embarrassed and wanting to get out of there as quickly as possible. I don't know how I regained my composure, but I just looked her straight in the eye and said, "I am not pregnant."

I'm not sure who felt more awkward at that particular moment, but the mother quickly became apologetic and didn't know how to respond. I wish I could say that this was an isolated incident, but unfortunately this scenario played itself out on several different occasions.

As time passed, my relationship with my friends and relatives became very strained and distant. Suddenly people seemed to not know how to relate to me. I don't think people meant to be not nice. I could sense their pitying expressions and maybe, subconsciously, this is why a distance was created between us. I sincerely believe that those previously close to me thought that they had my best interests at heart. Yet, even so, I felt extremely hurt and wondered how people didn't realize what they were doing.

Friends and family around me would be expecting and fail to tell me the news until I ended up hearing the information from other random people or seeing it for myself. I felt very much alone. "Why can't people just act normal?" I felt like shouting to anyone who would listen. "Don't people realize that I would be very happy to know their news? This is a very exciting point in their lives, and I would like nothing more than to share it with them even if I am not at the same stage of life as them."

I guess people felt that they didn't want to flaunt their berachos in my face. Why should they be the ones to tell me their joyous news when this special gift had not been bestowed on me yet? They didn't see how this logic was twisted. As a result, previously warm relationships became much more estranged. If you can't act naturally with someone and feel like you can't open up completely with the other person, you're not going to want to spend so much time together. This causes you to ultimately drift apart. This occurred with many of my dear family and friends.

Hashem, though, is constantly looking out for us even if we don't always realize it. I am very thankful for some of the friends He sent my way who were in a similar situation to mine. It enabled me to have someone to share my frustrations with. It suddenly seemed that I was not alone. There were other people who were having these inconsiderate moments as well. Somehow this just made me feel human again.

I always felt that if only I could say something to people in order for them to understand what I was going through, then maybe they would change. Maybe others would be spared from these insensitive comments. Maybe they would understand how painful it is to hear a friend whine about how hard it is to have three children so close in age and how I am so lucky to have time to myself. If only they would realize how much I yearn to have a noisy house filled with children. I would gladly give up my "time to myself" in order to have what she was complaining about.

After a year of waiting, my husband and I decided it was time to make an appointment with a doctor and discuss our particular situation. The doctor was very comforting. She assured us that we were very young and had plenty of time to have children. After filling out a questionnaire and a blood test, the doctor figured out that I have a condition that makes it difficult to have children. She advised me to lose weight and I was put on metformin, a drug usually prescribed to diabetics, but had also helped women diagnosed with my condition.

I went to see a nutritionist and tried my best to lose some weight. Weight had always been a struggle for me, and I found out that many people with my particular problem find it very difficult to achieve and sustain significant weight loss. It was slightly comforting to know that there was a reason that I had always had issues with dieting.

Baruch Hashem, after six months I got the great news that I was expecting, and we were ultimately blessed with a beautiful baby girl. I must say that I appreciate her with every passing day and realize what a true berachah has been sent to me from Shamayim. I am only sorry that not everyone has received this berachah yet, but I hope and pray that with time everyone longing for a child, or whatever his or her personal prayer is, will be answered by the One Above as quickly as possible.

I have learned to accept that I most probably will not have a house filled with eight, nine, or ten children, but obviously this is not my tafkid in life. Hashem has other plans for my bayis ne'eman b'Yisrael. Yet I must admit that it does get hard sometimes to come to terms with the reality of my situation, especially when friends married for as long as I am are expecting their third or fourth.

After having a child, I ignorantly believed that I could finally escape these painful comments. However, people still at times do not seem able to totally relate to me. The other day I invited someone over for a Shabbos meal.

Instead of politely declining or coming up with some excuse or another, the woman told me her true feelings: "My husband and I try to go to families that are a bit 'livelier,' if you know what I mean. We once went to a family who had just one child, and it was far too quiet with awkward silences."

I was flabbergasted and didn't know what to say. How should I have replied? My husband later tried to calm me down and explained to me that what this lady said was completely ludicrous and that I should not take the comment to heart at all. But how could I not? Did she really believe what she was saying? And even more so, how did it help to tell me about it?

I understand that people sometimes are uncomfortable when they meet someone who is different, especially if they feel they can't relate to that person. I think, though, that people need to learn how to be conscious of people's differences and treat them with sensitivity, but not with distance and awkward discomfort.

Our daughter is the highlight of our life. We realize that we are able to give her a lot more attention than we would have in a larger family. We are all very close and have a beautiful family connection. This is one of the many berachos that Hashem has sent our way.

Having only one child — in a society where big families are the norm — was definitely not what I imagined my family would consist of after almost nine years of marriage. Yet, when these thoughts arise, I remind myself that in a larger family sometimes kids can get lost and their parents are not able to be as attentive to their individual child's needs. This is something that we definitely do not have a problem with. I notice that kids enjoy coming to our home and like the fact that we are more hands-on and are able to give them more attention.

I do daven that I will be zocheh to have more children, not only for myself, but also for my daughter. Yet I have come to realize as life goes on that this is my personal, unique life challenge, gift-wrapped and tailor-made for me from Hashem. Only He knows what is ultimately good for me, and I need to concentrate on the many wonderful things that I do have. By dealing with this nisayon properly, I will fulfill my ultimate life mission. Hopefully, we will all reach sheleimus with the life challenges Hashem has sent our way.

What to Expect When You're Not Expecting
● Sara Mayer*

Eight days after my own wedding, I found myself at the same hall with the same friends eating the same food and listening to the same band. My husband and I laughed about it afterward. The entire evening was like a replay of our own simchah. For the other couple, our wedding had been a preview of what was to come.

Eleven months later, I stood at the bris of the same couple's new baby. There, in the back of the hall, I stood beside another friend of mine who had been married the year before me and was also waiting to celebrate her next simchah. I blinked back the tears that threatened to erupt at any moment. "We were married eight days apart! I could have had a baby already," I whispered to her.

She smiled sadly and squeezed my hand. "I could have had two."

Later, I confided in a friend the mixed feelings I had had at the bris. "I am so happy for her. But I feel such a loss for what I could have had. Why wasn't I blessed with a child?"

She absently stroked the hair of her toddler (born one year after her wedding). "But you're so lucky! You got this year to really work on your relationship with your husband. We spent most of our first year preparing for the baby."

I nodded, feeling unconvinced. The empty feeling in the pit of my stomach didn't make me feel very lucky.

<hr />

The waiting. The wondering. The constantly renewed hopes and the terrible disappointments. At work, they whispered knowingly behind my back any time I felt under the weather. My friends would nod and wink at each other whenever their suspicions were aroused. Everyone expected to hear the news soon enough. Only my husband and I knew that no news was forthcoming.

Did the pain control my life? Not at all. My friend was right in a way. There is so much going on in shanah rishonah that you have no time to dwell on infertility. As a new wife, you're busy setting up the house, settling into a new family, and getting to know your new life partner. But every time another month passes, the emptiness returns. It's unfair to measure infertility in years. This nisayon is counted in months.

We began to think about doctors but learned it was too early. "One year is normal and natural," we were told. "Just give it some more time."

Time? I seemed to have plenty of it. As the months passed, I became quite comfortable in my new role as a wife and daughter-in-law and began to crave something more. I often felt such deep disappointment and sadness: This wasn't supposed to happen! Everyone was so busy with diapers, strollers, cribs, and the delicious gurgling babies. Everyone, that is, except me.

Eventually the doctors began to take us seriously. The process of diagnosis can be frustratingly slow. My husband and I navigated our way through the tests and procedures praying for an end to it all. In the end, I was glad we had waited to see a doctor until after our first year. I don't think I could have handled the intrusion on my married life when everything was fresh and new. Infertility takes one's life and puts it under a magnifying glass. The doctors transformed me from hopeful wife to exposed patient. Even something as simple as taking my temperature every morning turned my life into a science experiment. When we moved on to daily injections and unpleasant procedures, it only got worse.

But life went on. I still needed to go to work every day. I dealt with the well-intentioned, well-meaning, but completely insensitive comments as best as I could. I attended the simchahs of others with a smile on my face that only faltered whenever another guest looked at my middle, clucked her tongue, and said she hoped to hear good news from me very soon, too.

It was four years until I held my baby in my arms. I remember the first sleepless night with my daughter. I thanked Hashem for the opportunity to have circles under my eyes. The time I waited allowed me to appreciate the blessing of children that much more.

I think the most important advice I could give to a woman just beginning this journey is to get support. Connect with other women going through this nisayon. Search out A TIME or some other organization that can assist in navigating the world of rabbanim, doctors, and clinics.

My journey was a lot easier once I knew I wasn't alone. In shanah rishonah, I found myself thinking over and over, Is this normal? Am I normal? I wish I had known about A TIME earlier in my journey so that I could have approached someone to get a clearer picture on what needed to be done. Even in that first year when it is normal to not be expecting, it's good to have someone to turn to for questions.

Navigating the Stares

●*Shoshana Borenstein**

I got lots of stares during my shanah rishonah. I am not very tall and I gain weight easily. Friends and acquaintances often asked me, "Are you...?"

"No," I'd be forced to answer, "I've just gained a little bit of weight. That's common in the first year of marriage."

This is what I was often told by friends who had just brought home a beautiful pink or blue bundle from the hospital: "I want to pray for you. Can I have your Hebrew name?"

It was nice that people wanted to pray for me and that they showed such an interest in my life. After all, friends are people who care about you. It can never hurt to have someone pray for you. But here's the not-so-pleasant reality: my lack of children was (and still is) none of their business.

It seems that in most of our communities, the dream is to get married and have kids right away, give or take a few months. Yet the reality is that not every frum woman will have a baby right away. Not every frum woman is well enough to have a child right way.

I find that when I tell people I do not yet have children, they assume it's because I'm unable to have a child. But in my case, I have several conditions that have caused me to have to wait to have a child. There are many of us, and our voices are rarely heard in the frum community. Quite frankly, many of us don't want to talk about it.

I am so tired of being identified as a nebbach.

During my shanah rishonah, certain medical conditions kept me from being able to have children. My rabbi and physician both agreed that I should not yet have a child.

We all know that chesed begins in the home. Before we can take care of another human being, we must take care of ourselves. In a marriage, especially during shanah rishonah, we must solidify the foundation of our marriage: — our physical and mental health as well as our relationship with our husband.

Children bring us closer to Hashem because we are always giving to them just as He always gives to us. However, there is no way to give to them properly and care for their needs adequately if we are unable to care for ourselves — or are in the process of learning how to do so.

Don't get me wrong. I am not waiting until some unspecified moment to have children. I am not waiting to make my millions before I move on to motherhood. I am waiting because halachah, based on the medical reality, has determined that I need to wait to become a mother. Please G-d, when the time is right.

This is why I am not a mother yet, and this is why my shanah rishonah did not include children.

I'd like to use this opportunity to give some chizuk to other women in my situation and to the people who love them:

1. *Just like Hashem brought you the "right person at the right time" — your husband — He will also bring you a child at the right time. Hashem controls the world. When someone asks for your Hebrew name so that she can pray for you, it can hurt, but let the person do this mitzvah. It can never hurt to have someone speak to Hashem on your behalf! We all know the power of tefillah.*

2. *Enjoy this time with your husband. You have the opportunity to spend more time with him. If you can, learn together. Take more walks together. You will certainly grow even more when you have children, but cherish every moment you have with your spouse.*

3. *Not all people who don't have children have tons of free time, but use the time you have wisely. Help others. Perhaps volunteer to babysit for a friend so that she can have more time with her husband or cook a meal for a new mother in your community.*

4. *Comments regarding a sudden gain of weight during shanah rishonah are inappropriate and rude. It doesn't matter who makes the comment. I had to confront a single friend who made some comments about my weight gain during shanah rishonah. She said something along the lines of "Do you have something to tell us?" I told her that even though she meant well, she embarrassed me as she had said this in the presence of others. Recognizing the error of her ways, she apologized.*

5. *My husband's grandmother says, "It's a shame that they can't have any kids yet." People will believe what they want. You don't have to tell your story to everyone as I did here. It's your choice. Don't let others judge you. There is only One True Judge in this world.*

6. *Of course, any decisions in this regard can only be made in consultation with a Rabbinic authority. Also, have a trusted friend or mentor that you can speak to about these matters.*

Finally, you are not a "nebbach." Self-pity and blindly accepting the pity of others will not bring you back to health and closer to children. Be happy with who you are and where you are in life. Thank Hashem for what you do have, not what you don't! After all, the one who is rich is one who is happy with his portion. If your recipe for life includes a dash of thanking Hashem for all the blessings you have, then your future child will be the cherry on your "cake of blessings."

Chapter 9

Demystifying Mothers—-in-Law

There is a potentially nerve-racking time that occurs in every *kallah*'s life. The moments between engagement and marriage, as well as the first few months that follow the *chuppah*, can be intense, to say the least. One of the challenges at this time is that in your head you are still figuring out not only what it means to be married but also what it means to change your status from single to married and from daughter to daughter-in-law.

Many *kallah*s spend much of their lives dreaming about the blessed day when they will become "the wife of..." However, the idea of becoming "the daughter-in-law of..." is the part of the package that is most often either not thought of at all or feared and dreaded almost as much as a visit to the dentist. Everyone hopes for a good *shvigger*, and some are lucky enough to get one. But even the best mother-in-law isn't your mother, so there are bound to be adjustments.

Some women think that they married their husband, not their husband's family. *What's the big deal?* they ask themselves. *We'll only see each other on Pesach and the occasional family simchah.*

For many, many marriages, however, in-laws can be a crucial part of the equation. Whether you live near each other or not, in some cases mothers-in-law can even be the most challenging part of a new marriage. While you are still busy trying to find your way around your new relationship with your husband, there is now another new relationship to navigate with far fewer clearly defined guidelines.

Having a mother-in-law can be an exceptionally beautiful thing or an exceptionally challenging one. The attitude with which you choose to enter the new family can make a big difference. Creating a relationship with your mother-in-law that is to succeed is extremely important. A big part of this success can be attributed to learning your mother-in-law's expectations for the two of you as the new couple and trying to be honest about your own expectations of your mother-in-law.

Take into account each other's backgrounds and cultures. The more you tread gently in the beginning while you're still learning each other's hot spots, the more comfortable your future Pesach Seders will be.

The following are stories from some of the best women I know, sharing their experiences, wisdom, and insights into the world of mother-in-law-hood. I hope you gain insights into your own mother-in-law from these pieces and will develop the best relationship possible with one of the most important people in your new life.

Good luck! It's worth the effort.

From Dream to Reality

● Batya Jacobs

She was working for a year, helping out in our kindergarten. Once, she had been one of the little girls in our neighbor's family. Now she was a young woman, a bas Yisrael ready for shidduchim. I was her boss. As I watched her with the children and with the kindergarten teacher, a little idea started hop, skip, and jump around my mind. Wouldn't it be nice if my former neighbor's daughter (for we had moved away) and my eldest son... You get the idea, I'm sure.

Well, the year went on, and my little idea would not be quieted. The more I saw of this sweet young lady, the more I wanted my fantasy to be real.

Nah! All mothers of eligible boys dream that every eligible girl will be the one. What are you going to do about it? How could you do anything about it?

I was too shy to even try out my idea on a few close friends to see what they thought. Day by day, week by week, the year rolled on. They, he and she, even saw each other sometimes, not deliberately, mind you, just on the odd occasion when their paths crossed. So I would see them and imagine. Oh, well, if it's meant to be, it will be.

The year was drawing to a close when a friend of mine said, "Don't you think those two are just made for each other? They even look alike."

"Brilliant idea. What happens next?"

"Oh, I don't know. My kids are still too young for that sort of thing."

I, too, had thought that my children were a bit young for that sort of thing. What mother of older teenagers really jumps enthusiastically into the shidduchim stage? This was my bechor. I hadn't dreamt that he was ready to up and marry. I was still into building the family and filling up our house. I wasn't ready to start emptying it out just yet.

Funny, that it was I who first thought what a sweet pair my son and my former neighbor's daughter would make. Yet when faced with the idea of marriage and leaving home — whoa...that was another story!

So I let another week or so slip by until I realized that we were preparing for the end-of-year party.

Face it, old pal, said a voice in my head, if you don't do something now that little dream won't come true.

Righty ho, old bean, I answered back, but you do realize that means we're talking weddings, daughters-in-law (tremble, tremble), and leaving home. . .

You want them to stay at home forever?

Yes — I mean no — I mean, I empathize with Peter Pan.

Well, all you need to do is do nothing and you will delay the inevitable.

But she seems such a perfect match.

Up to you, as they say.

That very night, I phoned one of my friends in my old neighborhood. "Could you do me a huge favor?"

"If I can."

"Could you perhaps ask the Bournstein family if their daughter would be interested — you know, if they're interested in my oldest son for their daughter, that sort of thing?"

"Oh! How exciting. Of course I can. I don't believe it. How they have grown up. Yes, yes, I'll ask them as soon as I can."

The family was interested, and after the usual checks and double checks the couple met and met again with the help of their go-between. Then they started arranging their own meetings. Not so long after that, they asked us parents to sit together and work out terms. They "closed," as they say in the vernacular.

The vort was a beautiful affair on a balmy summer's night in a pretty, well-lit garden. Sounds like a happily-ever-after, doesn't it? Then, suddenly, there was tension in the air. Suddenly, the dream seemed to waver.

"She's not sure," we were told.

So I spoke to her. "You, the mother-in-law, spoke to her?" I can hear you asking. Well, I'm not the most conventional of people. And I had built up a relationship over the year she had worked here. Not a special relationship. She didn't confide in me; we didn't have long chats like kindred souls. Just an ordinary working relationship based on mutual respect and, at least on my side, liking.

When I heard that she wasn't sure, my heart went out to her. I suddenly realized what an enormous and frightening task she was taking upon herself. I wanted to share my thoughts with her. Not to persuade her to "take the plunge," but to help her see all the sides. To put some stepping-stones in that torrent of confusion that she had fallen in. She was a sweet bas Yisrael in a quandary, and I thought I could be of some help. So I asked her if I could talk to her.

I was very tentative, not wanting to impose, not wanting to add to her burden. "These things happen," I said to her in a soft voice. "When the reality that you are getting married hits, it's mind blowing. The reality is that if you are engaged, then sooner or later you will be getting married. If you are going to be married, then you will cease to be a single, unencumbered girl living at home and letting the responsibility rest with your parents. You will be taking on your own life. Spending your spare time with your husband and not, or at least not so much, with your friends. The reality sometimes hits right between the eyes and the feet grow icicles."

So we talked all around the subject, she and I. We went out on a long, long walk and we talked: about marriage in general, about her hopes, about possibly being too young, about the boy (my son), about this and about that. Then I wished her all the very best and went home.

The process started again. They met again. We all held our breaths. Would they, wouldn't they? Baruch Hashem, they decided it was on again. Did our talk have any influence? She undoubtedly confided in her mother; they are very close. She probably went to her friends and mentors. Perhaps all she needed was time. What does it matter why? The invitations went out.

And then came the chuppah. My son said, "Harei at..." The glass was broken and "Daughter-in-law," I said to my new daughter-in-law.

"Mother-in-law," she said to me.

And we flung our arms around each other.

Our connection has grown over the years. We care about each other, respect each other, and enjoy each other's company. The first time the thought entered my mind it was a dream, and now I am grateful for the daughter-in-law I have and that my dream turned into this delightful reality.

Realizing What It Is to Be a Mother-in-Law

● Raizy Schwartz*

Somehow in my head I had the idea that a mother-in-law is synonymous with "difficult." I had heard horror stories, and I didn't see any reason my relationship with my mother-in-law would be any different from what I had heard the typical mother-in-law/daughter-in-law relationship would be.

I knew the picture in my head wasn't what I wanted. Being the assertive person I like to think I am, standing in my future mother-in-law's kitchen and helping her ladle out chicken soup, I said to her, "I really want us to have a good relationship. What can I do to make that our reality?"

She looked at me, and the words that left her mouth surprised me and delighted me simultaneously.

"Of course we are going to have a good relationship. You're marrying my son. You're going to take care of him for the rest of your lives. I'm grateful to you."

Honestly, her perspective had never occurred to me. To me, mothers-in-law had a stigma attached to them, that they had something against the woman who would "take their son away from them." In that moment, I realized that she was giving him to me with love. With that gift, she was also welcoming me into the family and saying she trusted me with her most prized gem.

As much as I thought I understood my mother-in-law and that we were in a good place, which we were, and baruch Hashem are, I didn't have a clue what my mother-in-law must have gone through when we got married until my own son was born.

After waiting anxiously for four years, my precious bechor arrived. When I held my little boy in my arms, I started to have the slightest clue of what it must be like to be a mother-in-law.

As my son grew, I understood my mother-in-law in a new way. By the time he was six months old, I started davening for his kallah. Please, Hashem, let her want to be a part of our family. Please let her love him with her whole heart. Please let her love me, too. And let me love her, not because she is my son's wife and I have to, but because we have a real connection and truly like and enjoy each other.

I know it sounds crazy davening for a wife who won't enter the picture for twenty years or so, but it's that *important to me. I know how much I love my son and how much I always want him to be a part of our lives. I know that who he marries is an integral part of that. I daven the way I have seen my mother-in-law daven for shidduchim for her children. She knows full well that a spouse will affect her child's course and that it's a blessing to be able to bring a daughter-in-law into your family.*

I won't say that my mother-in-law and I have everything in common or that we have never had a disagreement about how something needs to be handled. But I realize that we both only want what is best for her son — my husband. We are on the same team every minute of every day. I am grateful for the opportunity she afforded me in marrying her son. I hope to make her happy and proud for the rest of my life. I am eternally grateful to my mother-in-law for giving life to my husband, for rocking him through five months of colic, and, as I like to joke, for not giving him away in his teenage years.

It is because of her that I am married today and have a wonderful father for my children. I try to keep that in mind. I try to thank her and let her know I appreciate what she has done for me as a mother-in-law and for everything that she did for my husband before we ever met. I constantly remember that it is because of how she raised my husband and approved of our marriage that I am married today.

From Tears to Laughter

● *Faigie Heiman*

The fourth of five children, I was a spoiled child. My eldest sister vacuumed carpets on Friday. My second sister helped in my father's grocery store. And my job was crawling underneath the dining-room table or along the bottom of the long marble-topped buffet to dust the heavily carved, polished wooden legs. But we were unwanted help in Mamma's small kitchen. She didn't have the time or patience for the mess "help" created in her domain.

"Don't worry. You'll have plenty of years in your own kitchen," she'd say. "Go do your homework or read a book," and she'd shoo us out of the kitchen.

My mother's anti-kitchen-duty-for-daughters policy produced predictable results. One of my older sisters prepared a cup of tea for her soon-to-be husband without boiling the water; mildly hot water seemed fine to her. My eldest sister stored paper bags in her oven. The first time she tried baking she didn't know that paper bags should be removed when lighting the oven. The fire department taught her that lesson.

As for me, when I married I had a lot to live up to in the cooking department. My mother-in-law was a five-star housekeeper. Her food was far better than any magazine recipe, deliciously edible and beautifully presented. Her table settings and menu repertoire added mountains of fear to a daughter-in-law without any ability or basic knowledge of cooking. How I would ever fulfill the expectations of my husband and my family worried me constantly.

Thankfully, we spent our first summer as a married couple in a boys' camp, myself in the capacity of inexperienced camp mother and my husband as assistant head counselor. The upside was three meals a day served by a waiter, no food preparation, no dish washing, and no parents to roll their eyes in disapproval.

Then we moved into my in-laws' home in Baltimore for the month of Elul and remained there until we left for Israel after Succos. The first Friday we spent at their house my mother-in-law had an appointment at the sheitel-

macher. Before she left, she asked politely, "Faigele, please give Daddy some lunch. Everything is in the refrigerator. Just cut a tomato, take out the cottage cheese, and peel the cucumber."

After removing the tomato and cucumber from the fridge, I panicked. I had been born with two left hands and couldn't slice the tomato or peel the cucumber. I dropped the knife in the sink and ran out of the kitchen in tears. My father-in-law didn't understand what happened, and my husband humbly apologized and prepared the simple lunch for his father.

When my mother-in-law returned with her wig coiffed and her cleaning girl in tow, I stayed in our room, my eyes as red as the tomato I couldn't slice. None of my husband's comforting words helped. My mother-in-law felt sorry for me. I overheard her saying to her sister, "Poor Sholem. Can you imagine, his veibele can't even slice a tomato."

Inability to slice a tomato was only the beginning. Soon after we arrived in Yerushalayim, we lived in a run-down rooming house without any kitchen facilities, as rental apartments were unavailable. We were guests in a variety of homes, and when one of our hosts, Rebbetzin Chana, put a bowl of oranges on the table, she noticed that I didn't help myself. The rebbetzin took one golden orange from the bowl, arranged it on a single plate with a knife, and insisted that I taste it.

I had no idea how to peel or cut an orange. I was brought up on the nosh from my father's grocery store: potato chips, chocolate bars, devil dogs, doughnuts, and Pepsi. I'd never peeled an orange in my life! After the rebbetzin saw me slaughter her beautiful Jaffa orange, she patiently demonstrated orange peeling, one after another, until I finally got the hang of it.

Learning to cook, or at least preparing something hot to eat, started six months after we married when we moved into our first apartment. With the help of a neighbor, I learned to strike an Israeli mini-match without burning my fingers and then apply it to the gas without burning down the kitchen. Once I mastered that, it was Wednesday and my neighbor suggested that I buy fish. She also promised to show me how to prepare it.

I watched the fishmonger fish the carp out of the freshwater pool, hammer it on the head, slit its belly, and let the kishkes ooze out. Managing not to faint from the sight and smell, I carried it home wrapped in newspaper. I didn't have a shopping basket; I didn't know I was supposed to carry one. Paper or nylon bags were not part of Israeli shopping culture. Although the carp was dead, the innards were still writhing, and Malchei Yisrael Street witnessed a young American woman throwing a fish package in the air, screaming and running all the way home.

Cooking by instructions and recipes from the American Jewish Cookbook was worthless. I wasn't familiar with many ingredients, and besides, most of them were unavailable in our local Yerushalmi grocery. My husband was patient and tried to find ways and people to help me. Teary eyed, frustrated, and embarrassed, I felt as if everyone was laughing at my ineptitude. Yet success followed every few failures, and I learned how to make my way in the kitchen.

Two years later my in-laws visited to be there in time for the birth of our first child. They arrived before Rosh Hashanah and stayed until after Succos.

Rosh Hashanah preparations for my in-laws' first visit was enough to bring on labor. Trying to uphold American mother-in-law standards in Israel was a nightmare. The pressure of in-laws, new infant, and Shabbos and yom tov *preparations fed my low self-esteem. That first visit was one I can laugh about today, but I did a lot of crying then.*

Subsequent visits were better. I had learned to cook and bake competently and to entertain, and our visits together became a joy. Fear of my mother-in-law was gone; it didn't matter how she expressed herself, I knew she loved me. She wasn't well and needed a boost, and I was able to give it to her even if my pickled tongue was not as tasty, sharp, or sweet as hers, nor served with the same flair. I joked and asked her to touch it up, complimenting her while observing her every move. She gave me her recipe, which included "a bissele saltz" (a little salt) and "a bissele pfeffer" (a little pepper), and although I didn't know what "a bissele" constituted, the only tears I shed were when my in-laws left.

Fifty-some years on, I cry when I daven for good health, yet I always laugh at memories of my TLHS — Two Left Hands Syndrome. All beginnings are difficult, and mothers-in-law are not evil. They are set in their ways, as they've been there and done that for so many years, even if their sympathies are not always in sync with the younger generation's standards. The insecurity of a newlywed is so painfully natural, almost like childbirth. Just as each delivery leaves us wiser and more competent, the difficulties of first-time experiences with home, hubby, family, and in-law idiosyncrasies get settled in time. Maturity, understanding, and forgiveness are key players in resolving issues, and a sense of humor goes a long way.

On bad days, when a cake that I am baking burns and has to be discarded, I imagine my mother-in-law wrapped in a freshly starched apron reminding me, "Remember, Faigele, Rome wasn't built in a day."

Author's note: I have had the good fortune of eating in Faigie Heiman's home on both Shabbos and yom tov and can honestly say she is an amazing cook and an incredible homemaker and decorator. I have held her in my mind's eye as an example when I think of my personal goals as a balebusta. To think that her homemaking started with such a humble beginning is an inspiration.

The Mother-in-Law You Hope You Don't Get
Anonymous (Let's Just Call Me Mazal!)

Have you ever heard of the stereotypical mother-in-law? The one who is manipulative and deceptive? The one who goes behind your back and asks your husband to agree to things you have already answered no to? The one who uses guilt and attempts bribes to get you to do things you are not comfortable with? Well, this type of mother-in-law is not fictitious. She has a name: I call her "Shvigger."

My mother-in-law is not an easy woman. I should have realized this when she knocked down every sugges-tion I had for where to have our wedding. Then she tried everything in her power to convince us there was only one hall to have our wedding in, even if I hated the idea, but it was something I should agree to for the greater good of shalom bayis.

I should have realized that there would be problems when she announced our engagement party to her friends without checking if my family had the date free. I should have known something was up when she insisted on choos-ing my kallah teacher, where I should get my dress, which invitations we ended up with, who our caterer would be, and where all of our sheva berachos would be held.

There were many times I should have realized just how difficult a woman my mother-in-law-to-be was, but I was so busy focusing on how wonderful her son was, I *didn't take anything she said or did to heart. I had heard that planning a wedding was stressful. As stupid as it sounds now, I didn't realize that if this was how she acted before the wedding, I had a lot more in store for the future than I'd planned on. I tried to focus on the life I would build with her son, telling myself over and over that I was marrying him, not his family.*

Of course, I was wrong, and it took more than just shanah rishonah to figure that out. Now I tell women that they are marrying into a family, and one has to be realistic about that fact. But then, I was young and naïve. And my husband was so kind and good (as he still is, baruch Hashem).

Shanah rishonah is long over now, and as the years passed, I learned certain coping skills as well as proactive techniques to deal with the mother-in-law with which I was blessed. I can't say that my mother-in-law has changed dramatically. I can't say that I have either. What I can say is I have learned how to deal with her better.

The good news is that as more of her children have married, we are not nearly as much of the focus of her life as we once were. The reality, however, is she is still who she is and always will be. So I have developed strategies to try to make a difficult situation better.

My suggestions on dealing with a difficult shvigger — or, at least, what works for us:

- *When she is insensitive, or comes up with seemingly crazy plans for us, or says things that are hurtful, I try not to take her too seriously.*

- *My husband answers for us as a couple. When my mother-in-law asks me things directly, I say, "Ask Chaim. I'm happy to do whatever he says." As opposed to a time when I tried to protect him from her by taking the brunt. Now I warn him of what is coming and allow him to handle it. I realize he has a different connection with her and can say things to her that I can't.*

- *I remember why I'm grateful to her and forgive the rest as much as possible. I try to see her good qualities and appreciate the good things she has taught my husband. I compliment my mother-in-law for the things she really is wonderful at. She is a ba'alas chesed and a wonderful cook. She has passed on some amazing recipes and taught the trait of chesed to my husband.*

- *I try to remember that the same Hashem Who made my husband for me gave me this mother-in-law, and He didn't necessarily make her according to my specifications. The issues I have to deal with come and go in waves. Even if it feels awful one day, in a few days or minutes it can pass. Then she will leave us alone for weeks or months at a time.*

- *My husband was raised by this woman. When he slips into negative family patterns, that isn't entirely his fault but how he was trained in childhood (we can all learn healthier communication skills).*

- *I have realized that Hashem gave me this mother-in-law, and this is a test that may take years, but with Hashem's help, I can pass.*

- *I try to remember that she is doing the best she can and respect her according to halachah.*

Mothers-in-Law Have Feelings, Too
—————————————————————— • Cookie Attias

Before my wedding, my mother took me aside to talk to me. Being a kallah, I could only imagine what she wanted to say. My thoughts went off to all kinds of possibilities: about being a queen and making your husband a king and, of course, to let me know that she would always be available to me. All this I already knew. So what did she want to talk about?

"Cookie, love your mother-in-law more than you love me. I already know that you love me, but she doesn't know that you love her."

Well, for once in my life, I kept quiet and let those words sink in. Truth be told, I never knew that there could be such a problem. I remember my grandmother coming to visit us every Sunday. There were never any disagreements, and my mother never said anything bad about my grandmother, her mother-in-law.

Unfortunately not one member of my husband's family could attend our wedding. His family lived in Israel, and the wedding was in Chicago (in those days traveling between Israel and the United States was not so easy or common as it is today). I remember feeling sadness for my husband that his parents couldn't attend the most important milestone in his life.

Two years after we were married, we had enough money to visit my in-laws. My husband hadn't seen his parents in nine years. He had left home in Morocco as a boy to learn in a yeshivah in London, then went to the Lakewood Yeshivah. We met in New York when I came in for a friend's wedding, and we got married in my home-town of Chicago. He was now on his way to see his parents for the first time in years. And he was bringing along a wife.

It's a strange feeling meeting your mother-in-law for the first time, but especially after two years of marriage. What will she think of me? Will she like me? Will she be happy with her son's choice? How will I talk to her? Will I truly be able to love this stranger? What should I call her? What should she call me? My nickname, Cookie? My

Hebrew name is really a Yiddish name, Mina Raizel. Will it be strange to her, coming from Morocco?

We were greeted in my in-laws' house like a royal couple. Besides my husband's parents, all his siblings and nieces and nephews were there. I'm sure you've heard that a son usually marries someone similar to his mother. Well, in my case, it was just the opposite. She was dark; I was light. She was Moroccan; I was American. She was quiet and I wasn't. She liked Moroccan music and I liked semi-classical. She spoke a Moroccan Judeo-Arabic and I spoke English. She didn't like the color black, and I thought it was elegant. (When we finally did move to Israel and bought a car, we wanted the color black, but because we knew that we would be driving to visit her, we bought blue instead.)

The two things we did have in common were that we both had a broken Hebrew, and we both loved her son, and because of that we had a strong bond. She loved me and I loved her. I called her "Ima" and she called me "Binte" (my daughter).

Fourteen years into our marriage, we made aliyah and I got to know my mother-in-law much better.

As I was a working wife and mother, my husband would help me with the chores in the house. We could never tell that to my mother-in-law because she felt that her sons should never do those kinds of things. Once she was staying at the home of one of her sons, and she saw him take out the garbage. She didn't say anything to her daughter-in-law, but the next morning she got up much earlier than the rest of the family and took out the garbage herself. When she would come to spend Shabbos with us, my husband would say, "Quick, let me help you finish up before Ima comes." It made her happy to know that her sons were treated well, and we never wanted to disillusion her.

Life seems to have whizzed right by. My in-laws are surely in Gan Eden. I am so happy that my relationship with them was good, and I have no regrets. I hear so many in-law jokes and stories, and I think people forget that in-laws have feelings and are people, too.

I've since become a mother-in-law. I used to worry about what my in-law children would think of me. And I look back and think that when I met my mother-in-law, she must have been wondering the same thing. Would she still have a connection with her son? Would he be loved and taken care of? Would he be appreciated? Would I be able to call her Ima or Ma or Savta, and would she be able to call me "Binte"?

I often think of my mother-in-law, her quiet way, her kindness, and her Old World charm. She is missed by all of us. May her memory be blessed.

The Mother-in-Law Thing

● Judy Caspi

You are still starry eyed and full of the memories of your wedding day. Your life is a constant parade of new feelings, new experiences, and new situations. You are finally on your own with your wonderful new husband, ready to stake out a life together. As an engaged couple, there never seemed to be enough time to fully discuss all the important details of life after marriage. And now that it is here, in your lap, you want it to be perfect.

The thrill of being on your own, starting a new life, and making your own way has filled your dreams. But your waking hours may bring you face-to-face with a different reality. An apartment to keep clean, meals to make, laundry! Does every bride feel so overwhelmed?

Sometimes you just want to yell, "Help!" but who will hear you? You find it hard to explain to your unmarried friends and you're too embarrassed to be the one to bring it up when you get together with the other new kallahs. Besides, it doesn't seem possible that anyone else is going through this.

There is also another challenge that no one ever warned you about before the wedding. Your mother-in-law. His mother. The woman who molded, trained, and educated her son — your husband — to her very own particular specifications. He is her most precious creation, and you have taken him away from her, forever. Never again will she be loved so unconditionally. She knows that life as she knew it is now over. But that doesn't prevent her from wanting to maintain a special connection to her son's new phase of life. After all, up until now, she was his constant companion through all of the other stages. She is not about to give that up.

She strives to be a relevant and meaningful part of your lives. Don't you know that Shmulik likes his shirts on hangers, not folded? After they have been ironed, of course. And his very favorite dish is not tuna salad on rye. Did he really tell you that? Such a sense of humor, my Shmulik has. You know the true answer is braised brisket of beef. He never mentioned it? You wait, he will. Better yet, you should surprise him and make my recipe. Shmulik licks his fingers every time he eats my beef. This recipe comes from my mother, may she forever rest in peace. He'll love you for it. Trust me. Got a pen ready to write it down now?

And on it goes, until you feel yourself entrenched in the most difficult position of being in the middle, between your husband and his mother. You are torn between sticking to tradition and starting new traditions with your husband. The old patterns worked for generations, but now the world has changed, along with the way you think. You find yourself wondering, Should I toe the line?

Go along with everything his mother says? Why does life have to be so complicated?

You learn to pick and choose. You find your way by trial and error. You realize that you can agree to everything your mother-in-law says and then do it your own way. You learn to take her advice with a pinch of salt.

I remember hearing my own late mother-in-law slaving over a hot stove in the early hours of the morning, when I was barely awake. (Yes, my shanah rishonah was spent in large part living with my new husband and his parents, or living with my new husband and my parents!). What could she possibly be doing?

When the heady aromas of her tantalizing home cooking lured me out of bed, I saw she was preparing dinner. "Why now?" I barely mumbled over the steaming mug of coffee she placed in front of me.

"Make dinner first," was her answer. "No matter what your plans are for the rest of the day, always get supper ready before you go out."

Here was a piece of advice that I could accept or just as easily reject. But before I did either, I thought about it and how I could adapt it to my lifestyle. Maybe I could prepare the side dishes in advance. Or maybe get the salad cut up beforehand and season it at dinnertime. No matter how you looked at it, it was good, solid advice. And I felt empowered the minute I realized I could turn it around to suit my purpose. I had the ability to keep an open mind and adapt the useful bits of her wise words.

What worked well in one generation does not always make the grade in later years. If you pick what works for you, you can show your mother-in-law how adaptable you are. Your husband will see you as a person who respects her elders but has the confidence to make her own choices in running her household.

Early on in my marriage, I made a pact with my mother-in-law. I wanted her to teach me some of her ethnic family recipes. But I had two stipulations: it had to be food that I enjoyed eating, and it had to be easy to make. That way, my kitchen would be enveloped in those fragrances familiar to my husband since childhood without my slaving over a stove to accomplish them. Then, when he yearned for "something special," his mother was all the more happy to produce it for him knowing that this dish remained exclusively hers.

My advice, kallahs, is to jot down that brisket recipe. But check with Shmulik first before trying it out. Maybe he was only trying to make his mother happy! Or maybe he'd rather make you happy and take you out for dinner.

A Mother-in-Law's Advice

● Dina Solomon

Having raised seven sons, I am overjoyed that I now have many daughters: the women that they married. I enjoy the feminine presence in our home and at family gatherings, and I encourage my children to visit often.

When you marry into a new family, it's good to remember that you now form a team of two women who love your husband the most in the world. Do not set yourself up to be in a competition, but rather, take advantage of the power of two and become allies. A good first step is to clarify what your mother-in-law would like to be called.

I have some daughters-in-law who asked if they could call me Ima, and I find it very endearing. Some people may take a more formal approach and prefer to be called by the family name, and some may prefer a more casual arrangement and be on a first-name basis. You are entering into a new small society, and it's good to diplomatically research the customs and preferred behavior of the family.

I would suggest never using your mother-in-law as a confidante on the flaws of your husband. Do not expect a mother to side with you against her "tzaddik" of a son. Once you have formed a strong relationship, you may ask for advice, but understand that your mother-in-law may not always wish to be involved in the details of your marriage. Generally, it's a good idea not to discuss details of your marriage with your mother-in-law.

In my experience, most people desire closeness, compassion, and understanding, so reach out by calling or e-mailing if you live far away. Take note of your mother-in-law's birthday and give her recognition in some small way. On the other hand, two of my sons live very close to our home, and it is important that we learned boundaries as well as always seek to keep harmony.

Bonding happens through shared experiences, both joyful and challenging. I had the privilege of being asked by one of my daughters-in-law to assist at the birth of her baby. We had not planned a home birth, but circumstances and the short duration of the labor found us together, sharing that ecstatic moment when the baby entered into the world. Now there is a deep level of trust and love between us, and these are the best qualities to strive for in any relationship.

If your mother-in-law has many daughters of her own, you will perhaps feel that you cannot get as close as you may like. Always be patient and let the passage of time and shared events forge a bond naturally.

If your husband came into the marriage from an unhappy relationship with his parents, or if there is stress in the home that he came from, perhaps you will be able to be a bridge for forming new closeness.

Grandchildren always seem to smooth the way and remove the chill from past difficulties. When your mother-in-law sees that her son is happy and growing in his life and in his middos, she will know that his marriage is good for him, and she will bless you and be grateful. You are the person who will share his life and help him to fulfill his potential. Take the job seriously and may you be blessed with womanly wisdom and success in everything you do.

Part 2

Advice From Women Who Know

The Wisest Women I Know Share Their Marriage Advice

Have you ever wanted to ask someone a question but felt it was not appropriate or just too personal? Well, I have felt that feeling many, many times, and it's always over the same topic: marriage.

I assume that if a woman is married twenty, thirty, or forty years and is still smiling, as a couple she and her husband must be doing something very right. So finally I got up my nerve. I made a list of the women I wished would enlighten me on the secrets to a good marriage, and I asked them to share their wisdom.

I formulated a few specific questions I could ask various women I respect who are in various stages of life and marriage.

First, I asked the following questions to women who had been married for over twenty years: What did you learn about marriage from your parents' marriage? What is it like when you argue? Is there any advice you'd like to suggest to newlyweds? What's the secret to a good marriage?

I feel personally blessed to have been able to learn from the experiences of these wonderful women. I hope you will enjoy their advice as much as I have and learn about your own relationship from the wisdom these women have shared.

The following are excerpts from interviews with women who have been married for twenty years or more:

—————————————• Moti Teitelbaum, married 41 years:

What did you learn about marriage from your parents' marriage?

My father was a survivor of the war. To him, if something was made well, he had no issue keeping it for twenty or thirty years. He had a coat. It was a good coat, but my mother hated it. She asked him to get rid of it, but he couldn't understand where she was coming from. It was a good, warm coat; there was nothing wrong with it. So it was old and out of fashion. That didn't matter to him. It was still in good shape, and there was no reason to get rid of it.

My mother was a fancy woman. Eventually she realized the coat wasn't going anywhere. So she asked him a different question: "Will you buy a new coat just to wear when we go out together?" My father had no issue with that. It wasn't that he wanted to embarrass my mother; he just didn't come from the same worldview she did.

After the war, if he had a slice of bread with butter and cup of coffee, my father felt rich. So to him, his coat was fine. But when my mother made that request of him, he heard her. They went out to the finest men's store around and bought a good expensive coat my mother could feel proud of when she was with my father.

That's what real love is. It's giving in even if you don't see yourself as wrong because you love your spouse and want to accommodate him or her. I always remember that story of my parents. They were very special.

What is it like when you fight?

We don't fight. It's different now. When you're young, you fight about your own kavod. How can he be so thoughtless? Why can't he even understand why this is so important to me? Why isn't he acknowledging me and my needs? It's hard to get over yourself.

When I was younger, I fought to establish who I was. Now, I know who I am. I don't have to prove myself or my point of view. I know my husband loves me, so I am not trying to get him to prove it. When you are older, your "self" doesn't enter the picture as much; it's a different self, a bigger self. When you are older, it blends into something else.

Fighting when you are young is like a volcanic explosion. Things build up and then they explode. But think about lava. After the volcano explodes, the lava flows down the mountain. At first, when it is hot, it destroys everything in its path. But as it travels down further and further, it cools, and eventually it is just volcanic soft ash: it melts and blends into something else.

By the time a fight cools down, you might realize that what you were fighting about wasn't really such a big deal. The problem is how much those heated words can destroy on the way down. It's important to work on *yourself until you change the way you go about things. Don't let things build up: don't allow for explosions in your life. Try to handle things when they are small and won't leave a path of damage in their wake.*

Is there any advice you'd like to suggest to newlyweds?

Over time, we learn communication skills. That's crucial. It can be very important to clarify that you are both understanding an issue or request the same way: "Am I to understand that you mean...?"

I also think it's crucial to put yourself in the other's shoes. Listen to how you sound. Would you like it if someone spoke to you the way you are speaking? Would you respond in a positive fashion and want to be helpful, or would you want to get out of there as fast as possible? Speak the way you would like to be spoken to.

—————————• *Rebbetzin, anonymous, married 49 years:*

What did you learn about marriage from your parents' marriage?

There's a story I like to tell: A mother is sitting in a room with a locked door. Her kids are banging and yelling, "Mommy, Mommy, what are you doing in there?" As the woman sits eating breakfast, she answers her children, "I'm making you a mother."

There are times in life you have to make a mother for your children, and there are times in life you have to make a wife for your husband. You have to take care of yourself and make sure you are well rested. A person who isn't can't cope as well. It is in your family's best interests to take care of yourself.

What is it like when you fight?

We don't. Sometimes staying quiet is also very helpful. Don't answer right away, sometimes not at all. Sometimes things will blow over if you just don't react.

What's the secret to a good marriage?

The secret is that you want to have a good marriage, and you are willing to sacrifice for a good marriage: each partner has to give. When you want to win, you don't worry about the little things; if something is really bothering you, you sit down and talk about it even if your words could hurt the other person. You have to realize that you have the same goals. Both people in the marriage have to be willing to be mevater, to give up on their desires sometimes.

A person has to know how to act. How to be a "ben adam." If one doesn't have those skills naturally, one has to learn. Learn a good mussar sefer; I suggest Michtav MeEliyahu. And Rav Nissim Yagen, zt"l, used to say people should read the biographies of the gedolim to see how they lived. There are many stories about how gedolim treated their wives.

Marriage has to be a "give-give" situation. It may take longer for one partner to learn this, but it has to be that both partners are giving. Ultimately, you will get in return, but that certainly isn't why you give. You have to be a ba'al chesed in your marriage.

Is there any advice you'd like to suggest to newlyweds?

"Sorry" isn't a bad word. Apologize when you're wrong.

What did you learn about marriage from your parents' marriage?

The story of my grandparents. She was the daughter of a prominent maggid, and he was the son of a poor family but a huge talmid chacham. They each said the same thing when they heard of the shidduch. He said, "Why would she want me?" And she said, "Why would he want me?"

We are usually aware of our own ma'alos, our good points, but we have to realize that humility is important, and that we are just as imperfect as our spouse. At the same time, we have to overlook our spouse's faults.

We all tend to be very forgiving of our imperfections, our less-than-good parts of ourselves. That is the mitzvah of "V'ahavta l'rei'acha kamocha": to be as forgiving of others (especially of our spouses) as we are of ourselves. The same way we find mitigating circumstances for our own behaviors, we need to do so for our spouses.

Is there any advice you'd like to suggest to newlyweds?

We all need someone to bounce things off of, a third person. Find a "relationship mashpia"; a third person can keep you real about when it is time to give in and when an issue is real and important.

What did you learn about marriage from your parents' marriage?

I saw that my parents argued a lot, and I didn't want that. I think I found it attractive that I knew my husband well, and we wouldn't fight. He had good values, and we agreed on all of the main things in life.

What is it like when you fight?

In our lives, it wasn't necessary. It was a value to my husband that I got time to do the things that I loved and needed. My husband encouraged and helped me to develop myself in any way I wanted to. I studied one day a week for twenty years. Even when we had no money, my husband borrowed money from his parents so I could study, and he babysat while I learned, and we paid them back.

For a long time, I tried not to ever fight. Eventually, I realized that I did have to stand up for things that I really wanted once in a while. But it was a value to me that my children didn't grow up with fighting. When they finally did see us argue, they came and asked us to stop. They said it wasn't what they were used to. I explained to them that I had to stand up for my idea, but I clarified for them that when it was dealt with, it was over.

What's the secret to a good marriage?

In our case, we agreed to disagree. We could acknowledge our differences of opinion but not fight about them. For example, this has helped us a lot when it came to buying art. Instead of fighting over one picture, we bought two, when we could afford it. But we agreed on the big things so easily. Our children never ran from mother to father for different answers to the same question, thinking they could get a better deal from the other parent. We stood together on every decision connected to the children. Sometimes we might go to the other and ask, "Am I being fair?" Then we would rethink it.

"If this is important to you, we'll do it": that is a common phrase in our home. We know how to defer to each other. If something is the other's department, we know it and let that person handle it.

I see that the more people have in common, the easier marriage often is. On the basic things, it makes it so much easier. On the little things, I say to myself, Let it go. If there is a reason to support each other's reasons and suggestions, we support it. We like to agree with each other. We do, and we did, and we have, with and without money.

Does this sound so good because you are both just easygoing people?

My husband is easygoing. I am not.

Is there any advice you'd like to suggest to newlyweds?

My father-in-law told us to never go to bed angry. Also, we always tried to eat our meals together. We didn't only raise our children around the Shabbos table but at every meal.

We shared raising the kids and household responsibilities. He always did the dishes because he wanted our kids to see that. I think that had a lasting effect on the next generation. Now, all of my sons help their wives.

All the teaching we did for our kids was by example. We spoke nicely and respectfully to each other. Our children learned how to interact with other people, how to speak nicely, because that is the standard we set in our home.

What did you learn about marriage from your parents' marriage?

My parents divorced when I was young. So what I learned from them is that whatever your parents' marriage is like doesn't have to be yours. You don't have to recreate the home you came from.

What is it like when you fight?

It's not an issue. Not anymore. It's probably been ten years since we had a fight. Once the children are grown, it's so much less of an issue. It's different when you are raising children together. There is so much more to deal with. There's a certain point in marriage when you realize it's all water under the bridge. All of the things you could fight about, they're really nothing.

What's the secret to a good marriage?

There isn't one secret, but I think truth is really important. Honesty not just in day-to-day stuff but in who you are as a person. If you aren't honest about who you are in your marriage, in the long run you are going to suffer. If you aren't true to yourself, it can really cause problems.

Is there any advice you'd like to suggest to newlyweds?

As much as you have to be truthful, you don't have to give a running commentary on everything that happens in your marriage. Everything doesn't need or deserve a comment. Let's say taking out the garbage is an issue in a marriage. You don't have to get into it with your husband.

Even if you ask him to do the same thing a hundred times, you have to realize that he isn't trying to hurt you.

In marriage, there is a certain amount you have to absorb and let go. The small things I mean, like the garbage example. I am not saying that will be the thing, but every couple has their issues. When it is a small thing that is getting to you, ask yourself, "In the big picture, does this really matter?" Think about the answer before you react.

I remember my Rebbi once told me it's the little things that break up marriages, like forgetting to put the cap on the toothpaste. Find a way to get over the little things.

Also, realize it's not just you who is adjusting and letting go. Your husband is also dealing with things you do that are probably hard for him, even if he doesn't say so. Men and women are just different.

—• Ruth Hyman, widowed after 30 years of marriage:

What did you learn about marriage from your parents' marriage?

Total commitment. My parents went through some rough spots, but both of them diligently worked through them, always committed to maintaining their marriage.

What was it like when you fought?

When I was younger, our infrequent fights were just plain awful. As we grew in our marriage, I recognized them as incredible growth opportunities. They were still really hard to go through, but weathering the storm of the fight, each of us really listening to each other, always elevated our marriage in the end.

What's the secret to a good marriage?

Trust. Make your marriage a safe place.

Is there any advice you'd like to suggest to newlyweds?

Let go of the need to be "right." Get your ego out of it. "Try on" your spouse's point of view to understand how the situation looks from his perspective.

Your marriage is an entity unto itself. It needs to be nurtured. You are both vitally important to the whole. Your marriage is a precious, growing thing and must be treated as such.

———————————————● *Leah Golomb, married 36 years:*

What did you learn about marriage from your parents' marriage?

My parents never argued in front of the children. They always had a united front. You felt like when you talked to one you talked to the other. There was no manipulation allowed. The respect was the main thing. My father had a lot of respect for my mother and he impressed upon all of us that she was to be respected.

What is it like when you fight?

Usually we fight when one or the other of us is expressing our disappointment or hurt or when one of us makes an assumption. But we do, usually, agree to try to see it through to the end. I try to push through it until we both get to that place where we feel better or understand each other. We keep working on it until we work it out.

We commit to hanging in there until we both feel better. Usually one of us will use a little humor to speed up the process.

What's the secret to a good marriage?

Learn Torah together. That is my all-time number-one best piece of advice. Learning Torah together reminds you that it isn't only you or only him. It reminds you that Hashem is in charge. Also, try to do things that are fun together, develop interests together, spend time alone together learning how to communicate.

When you first get married and are learning the many aspects of being married, learn how to speak to each other. Even though you know you are soul mates, he doesn't know what you are thinking, and you don't know what he is thinking. Don't take anything for granted. I really appreciate when he understands me, and I try to encourage it by letting him know how much I appreciate that he understood me. That encourages him to get it right more often.

Is there any advice you'd like to suggest to newlyweds?

Daven for each other. Daven for whatever it is that you feel like you are missing. Ask Hashem to help. That is always helpful. Don't be afraid to humble yourself. Learn to be good friends; spend time together.

Hashem gave us a sense of humor. He put together a man and a woman, and you need some humor to get along.

What did you learn about marriage from your parents' marriage?

Actually, what I learned from my parents is that I can't be my mother because my husband is nothing like my father. I learned that my relationship with my husband is very different from my parents' relationship. And I realized I had to learn who I could be because I could not just become my mother. Their relationship was great for them, but for us a different relationship would suit us better.

What is it like when you fight?

We don't fight very often. I realize if the fighting isn't going to change anything, there isn't a point. Periodically, you have to let off steam, but really marriage is about acceptance. Think about what is really important. You have to accept who your spouse is, how he is. Accept your life as what Hashem is giving you. Acceptance makes a big difference.

What's the secret to a good marriage?

Enjoy being with each other and having respect for each other. And giving each other space to be who you are and not expect your spouse to be exactly like you, because he isn't going to be anything like you. Having special times together to really be there for each other, being close, thinking of the other's needs, and being open with each other is also imperative.

It's also important to pick your battles. I am not suggesting that you never say anything when something is bothering you, but you really have to prioritize when something is important. For instance, let's say your husband is very messy and you are very neat. Give him a space in the house where he can be messy. As for me, I realize that if I want to live in a neat house I am going to have to pick up after him sometimes, and that is a price I pay to live with him, and it is a small price to pay. If I wanted everything perfect, I could live alone, but who wants that! It is such a small trade-off for getting to be married to my wonderful husband.

I think that also you have to work hard at seeing his good qualities and appreciating them. If you focus on the bad, you are going to be unhappy, and everyone has bad qualities. Give each other space to be imperfect, especially during shanah rishonah.

Don't take anything as a given. Whatever he does — like washing the dishes — appreciate it and realize it is a gift.

Also, make sure you have time together. Even if it isn't always something you are so interested in doing, it is good to do something together. Have dinner together every night. You don't even have to talk, just be together. We always know that at the end of the day, we are going to sit down and be together. It's a very nice way of sharing space.

Is there any advice you'd like to suggest to newlyweds?

I guess to be patient and to know that marriage is a life-long process, and it isn't going to be perfect overnight. Getting to know each other, learning to live with each other, is going to take time and you need to be patient.

Thinking about your own needs and wants instead of trying to take care of the other person can also cause problems. Try to think of what your spouse needs and how to take care of him. Remember what is important in the big picture.

Chapter 11

The Dos and Don'ts of Marriage

After the amazing answers I received from the interviews, I had another idea. I decided to create a questionnaire in which I asked women who have been married between two and fifty years to combine the wisdom they have gained over the years with the wisdom they wished they had had in their first year of marriage. Each woman answered the following four questions:

1. What are the "dos" of marriage?
2. What are the "don'ts" of marriage?
3. What do you know about marriage now?
4. What do you wish you had known about marriage in *shanah rishonah*?

Again I found the answers amazing and helpful for any married woman at any stage. Interestingly, there were some similar answers or women who focused on the same topics. I decided to include those answers specifically to show how frequently the same issues came up and how different women dealt with them.

The Dos of Marriage

- Express your needs and don't expect your husband to intuit them. We speak a different language than our husbands do and miscommunication happens. Ask your spouse to make clarifications as needed. Don't give up your favorite portion for your husband's sake, only to discover twenty years later that he hates that portion and only accepted it because he didn't want to hurt you. Ask, talk, and don't rely on assumptions or hints. Learn how to communicate.

- Ask for help when you need it, and don't rely on him noticing that you need help. Try to bring up sensitive subjects after your husband has eaten, and only when you are relaxed with each other, not in the middle of a disagreement.

- Give your husband positive feedback when he needs it and even when he doesn't.

- Remember, the big C in marriage is compromise. Whenever you hit on a difference of opinion, the need to find that middle road is essential. It doesn't make everyone happy all the time, but it stops an argument most of the time.

- Respect your husband. Treat your spouse with more love, affection, and respect than anyone else. Find out what is important to your husband, and make it your priority.

- Give your husband respect. It's not a fifty-fifty relationship like the outside culture may have led you to believe. Each person must commit to giving 80 percent, and it must be done totally with *simchah*. Example: If you and your husband are sitting on the couch reading, and he asks you for a glass of water, the first reaction may be, "Hey, we're both sitting here reading, you're thirsty, and I'm not, so get your own water!" Wrong answer. I have learned to say to myself, *What a zechus to be married to this good-hearted person*, and aloud to him, "It would be my pleasure." Then I get up and get his favorite glass and put in ice and water, which is the way he likes it, and hand it to him with a smile. You know what? It makes a difference in the way he treats me! And daven a lot, all the time. Daven about your marriage, your children, your house, and your *middos*.

- Work on your own *middos*. *Middos* can only help in your marriage. Try to be the best wife possible with what Hashem has given you. Look at the good qualities of your spouse and try not to harp on the bad ones. Try to grow in *ruchniyus* and *gashmiyus* with your husband. Try to change yourself, not your husband. Always give the benefit of the doubt; find out the whole story before you jump to conclusions! Remind yourself that if you are kind to your spouse, you are being kind to yourself. Have patience, tolerance, selflessness, kindness. Don't be critical of your spouse. Smile. For problem-solving and good communication, ask your spouse, "What would work for you?"

- Encourage your husband to help you around the house from the beginning — taking out garbage, doing the dishes — so that by the time you have kids and things get hectic, he is used to helping.

- Spend time together.

- Remember the things you enjoyed before you got married. Continue to do those things. Incorporate them into your new married routine. Hold on to the things that make you happy.

- Take the time to find out what your spouse really likes and enjoys and do those things with him, even if you don't necessarily enjoy them. Even if my husband wants me to do things I don't enjoy, I do them because I know it makes him happy. And he is happy knowing that I do things for him since he knows that he does things for me. It's a delicate balance properly satisfying both parties!

- Have food available at all times — ingredients you can throw together to make a meal in under fifteen minutes.

- Laugh together. Go out on date nights, no matter what. Take vacations! Do apologize. If you are really angry, *go out*. Getting out of the house does wonders, allowing things to naturally pass. Spend time together with no agenda at all.

- Welcome your husband home with a warm and relaxed atmosphere.

The Don'ts of Marriage

- Don't store things up. Talk about things as soon as they start bothering you.

- Don't ever plunge head-on into an argument with your husband. Always try to put your own feelings and emotions aside, if possible, and try to see things from his point of view. Then find a way to tell him what is in your heart without alienating him. Don't blame him and especially don't build up expectations, realistic or not, only to be disappointed when he didn't really "get" what you wanted or meant. This is a person who grew up in a different environment, has different ideas on life, and has no way of understanding things in exactly the same way you understand them. If you are not too overwhelmed with emotion, try to stand in his shoes and see the situation from his point of view. Then speak to him in a way that will help him understand how you feel without the anger, guilt, finger pointing, and pain. Then he has a chance to be sympathetic for you and change what he can to make life better, more peaceful, and more joyful for the two of you. If there is something bothering you, make it clear what it is, and try to choose the right time to tell him about it, when he will be most able to hear it, and, hopefully, be sympathetic enough to act on it.

- Don't get stuck on personality stuff.

- Don't dwell on your husband's mistakes or flaws, or confront him with them. He knows he made a mistake when you told him once. Now he just needs you to make him feel good about himself. Criticizing only creates a tense atmosphere and makes him not want to be around you.

- Don't nag about something you have asked your husband to do. Our husbands will get to it when they get to it. We may live busy lives, but so do our husbands, and women are known for being better at multitasking.

- Don't try to educate him or be his *rav, rosh yeshivah*, or *mashgiach*. Don't try to change him into somebody you would like him to be. Don't think of your husband like you would your child, that you need to train him or teach him how to behave. Don't tell him what to do. You can suggest, mention how important something is to you, but the ultimate decision is his. Rather than trying to change him, be an example and work on your own *mid-*

dos. You cannot change any human being in this world except one: yourself. You can change your reactions to him, but not *him.* Your job is to help him grow within his space, using his *kochos* — not yours.

- Don't see the negative more than the positive, the cup half empty instead of half full. Don't dwell on the bad, and forget to see the good and the positive in your partner, the relationship, or whatever is happening between the two of you.

- Don't compare your husband to anyone else, as it will only make you dissatisfied with your own husband. And truth be told, you only see the exterior of someone else's husband, so you have no idea what is really going on in the marriage.

- Don't criticize or blame. Use "I" statements whenever possible. Men often think if we're struggling with something, we expect them — or they expect themselves — to solve the problem. Make it clear this isn't what you're looking for, that all you want is someone to listen.

- Don't bring up every offense your husband has committed when you are in the middle of a disagreement. Learn silence. It's not necessary to give a running commentary on everything he says. Don't take offense at the small things and try to ignore criticism.

- Don't demand and don't try to manipulate. It never works anyway and just creates resentment that will pollute future experiences.

- Don't make a big deal out of little things. If you can, forget it right away. He is probably unaware of any wrongdoing. Accept it as a *kapparah* and make up your mind to be extra nice. It works!

- Be careful about using your husband as a sounding board when you want to just vent. Of course, you can discuss your marriage with him, but venting about your friend who upset you may lead him, in his effort to support you, to encourage you to further harm your relationship with your friend. It may be wiser to call your local rabbi or *rebbetzin* to vent, or for serious advice.

- Don't be afraid to go to a very good rabbi or therapist if you need help. Or talk to an older friend or mentor who's been there and knows more.

- Don't take out your frustrations on your husband. When you come home upset and annoyed about anything that happened outside your home, don't take it out on him. He doesn't deserve it, and, in return, he will probably get annoyed with you for being angry with him. It's a vicious cycle that's completely unnecessary.

- Don't say, "No, I can do it. You don't have to help." Accept help when it's offered.

- Don't allow your job, friends, *chesed* projects, and community work to absorb so much of your energy that you end up shortchanging your family and marriage. Many people need the advice of a wise outsider who can take an objective look at the total picture of their lives and help them see where their real priorities should lie.

- Don't spend too much time on the computer. The computer can be really addictive even if it is used for kosher stuff. Spending too much time on *frum* websites or shopping sites will take away from quality time you as a couple should be spending together. It can also send a message to your spouse that the computer is more interesting and fun than he is.

- Don't let your appearance go in the house and then get dressed up to go outside. Fix up your face and clothes especially for your husband.

- Don't criticize your in-laws!
- Don't give up. Even if things seem hard, keep working at it. It's a worthwhile investment.

What You Know About Marriage Now

- Marriage constantly forces you to grow and change — hopefully for the better!

- It's work. But it's wonderful when you put in the work. When you communicate about difficult things, and you do the work, the results you reap are wonderful. G-d willing, you get what you put into it.

- Nobody is perfect, and life isn't always a honeymoon. It doesn't mean you have a bad relationship; it just means that sometimes it's work. Engaged life is fun, but it's not reality. Don't expect to be elated all the time. There are a lot of realities and issues you have to deal with in marriage; don't let them scare you. It's just part of life.

- Men and women are just *different*. He can't multitask. He's *not* wasting time on purpose.

- You can't ask your husband to do things differently or change his behavior; it's not fair to him and, truth be told, you have to learn that you just have to accept him and make the best of things! Stop bothering him about things you know he can't change.

- Everyone will annoy you at some point in time no matter how much you love them. Accept it and get over it, because chances are you can be just as annoying to them.

- Marriage is a magnifier; it makes the good better and the bad harder. How much better and how much harder depends on you and your spouse and how well you treat each other.

- Things are never what they seem. You never know what's going on behind closed doors in someone else's marriage, so it's best to only focus on your own. Don't think that someone else has it better than you, as you might not realize that your husband is ten times better. Obviously when you committed to your spouse you loved him and made a conscious decision to spend the rest of your lives together and build a *bayis ne'eman b'Yisrael*. Getting married was only the beginning. You need to constantly work on it, improve it, and make it better. Things change over the years, people change, and your marriage changes. You and your spouse need to be focused on growing together.

- When I get annoyed, I breathe deeply and let it go through me. If it's not important, it goes away. If it is important, it stays and I know it needs to be discussed.

- It's important for a woman to put great effort into keeping her husband happy.

- Marriage is about being together in all situations, no matter how stressful. Anything can be worked out with effective communication and *derech eretz*. Nothing is about "you" and "me." Everything is about "us."

- Some of the limitations you both have can be changed or improved, while others just need to be accepted. Sometimes you have to just work with what you've got and not expect that there will be more than that. Certain issues may require you to turn to others — a rabbi, rebbetzin, or therapist — for help.

- There is no perfect marriage. It's up and down. He is a mirror for what you need to work on and you are a mirror for him.

- The purpose of marriage is *tikkun,* fixing yourself and your relationship to be the best you and it can be.

- It's best not to know *everything* before marriage. Surprises — for better or worse — can be a plus. If we knew everything before, we might never marry. Marriage is all about plunging in (albeit with responsible caution), and then learning to live with one's choice of a life partner.

- Many years ago, at a close friend's twenty-eighth wedding anniversary, she shared with me something priceless. She said that people think you have to work on your marriage for a certain number of years, and then things get easier and it doesn't require so much work. It's not true, she said. Marriage is something a couple must work on all their lives. Just like *tzaddikim* have a stronger *yetzer hara* than *resha'im* (even though it doesn't look like that on the outside), good marriages are those that the couple works hard on all through their lives. If you want your marriage to be strong, put time, energy, and effort into making it strong: constantly improving communication, making each other happy, being happy and grateful when the other does something for you even if it's not exactly what you wanted, and working on your own *middos* to become a better person.

- Showing *kavod* to your husband is more important than being right.

- It pays to look away from minor and even not so minor annoyances. Build your husband up whenever you can. Make believe your father or *rav* had done or said such a thing. What would you do then? Aha!

- A good marriage is a dance in which you are always learning new steps. Try not to step on your partner's feet, but apologize if you do. Saying "I'm sorry" goes a long way toward fixing any disagreement. You don't always have to be right, even when you are. It doesn't matter in the long run. Count your blessings every day and appreciate all that is right with your relationship rather than focusing on what isn't. Don't make comparisons to other couples. No one knows what goes on inside another household.

What You Wish You Had Known in Shanah Rishonah

I have to start this section with a joke my rabbi in Berkeley, California, Rabbi Yehudah Ferris, used to tell regularly at his Shabbos table: A man marries a woman expecting her to stay exactly the same as the day he married her. A woman marries a man expecting him to change. They're both wrong.

- The first year of marriage is so important in establishing a pattern in your marriage.

- You can't get married expecting to change any of his qualities. You need to accept him for who he is.

- There are times when it helps to be reminded of why you chose your spouse. I started keeping a jar full of reasons why I married my husband, but not until after our first argument. I wish I had begun earlier.

- Men need appreciation and acceptance. Just love him and accept him for who he is.

- I wish I had known being married was a lot harder than I thought it was. It takes consistent, hard work to maintain a solid marriage. I also wish I had known more about my husband's need for space.

- I wish I knew then that my self-worth doesn't come from the paycheck I bring in or lack thereof but the quality of the family I raise.

- Focus more on spirituality and family harmony. Don't worry so much about money. Hashem provides.

- I wish I had known how to show my loyalty to my husband and my parents at the same time.

- Although I am, *bli ayin hara*, happily married, I don't know why I felt such a rush to get married. I believe that if you get married a bit older you are so much more mature, and the beginning of marriage can be so much smoother. I'm not trying to buck the trend of getting married at twenty. I'm just saying that if you don't find your *bashert*, that time can be well spent and there is a benefit as well.

- Having a good marriage is a process that takes many years of hard work as a couple and on an individual basis.

- Learn how to communicate more effectively. Sometimes years of holding something against your spouse can occur over one small incident that was a misunderstanding. Ask what is actually going on: what he meant by a certain action instead of just assuming that you know.

- I wish I had known better ways to encourage my husband to learn Torah instead of fighting, nagging, and cajoling. I have since learned the secret: If he's reading the paper, ask him to share his thoughts. If he's learning Torah, leave him alone and give him quiet. It takes effort, but it does work.

- I wish I'd realized that I'm O.K. and that I should never compare myself to anyone.

- From a very early stage, it's important to work on striking a balance between speaking up and being quiet.

- I wish I had asked for help early on instead of trying to be superwoman. I wish I had learned to overlook criticism and not be so sensitive. I wish I had discovered a positive outlook earlier in life. On the one hand, for most people it's *not* an investment in righteousness to keep quiet about things your husband has done that disturb or upset you. You may think that it's not worth making an issue over, but these things build up and create long-lasting pain and resentment. When something is no big deal, it's easy to discuss it in a friendly way, so it never becomes an issue. On the other hand, not everything needs to be shared. Saying whatever is on your mind can, in the long run, negatively affect the quality of the relationship. It's worth getting guidance on what to say and how.

Chapter 12

Let's Hear From the Husbands

What Husbands Have to Say About Shanah Rishonah and Beyond

According to the cliché, "Every good book must come to an end," but this book just wasn't ready to agree, not until a few weeks ago. You see, I thought the book was done. But then an important question came up, "What about the guys?" I'd spent so much time exploring the female perspective, it never occurred to me to ask the husbands what they had to say on the subject of *shanah rishonah* and beyond. The idea intrigued me, and I agreed to add this chapter.

Originally we thought it would be the last chapter in the book, but I realized it fit the best right here in the advice section. I can't tell you how grateful I am to the person who requested it and came up with the idea. Now that I have had the privilege of compiling these interviews, I know why the book couldn't have been complete without them. I learned a great deal from creating this chapter and I am very grateful to the men, many of whose wives also wrote for or were interviewed for this book, who agreed to share their thoughts on marriage.

Ironically, when the idea of a chapter from the men's perspective was proposed, I was worried. I thought, *It's a great idea, but men won't want to talk about this stuff. They won't want to tell me their challenges, or what they wish they'd known before they got married. They won't want to share their personal lives.*

But lucky for me, and for you, I couldn't have been more wrong. Once I compiled the list of the men I was interested in interviewing, not only was I shocked to discover that every man I asked agreed to be interviewed, I was also pleasantly surprised to see how much they wanted to share. Rather than one- or two-word answers, I got long, instructive replies. In writing this chapter, I learned new ideas not only applicable to *shanah rishonah* but to marriage in general.

To me, the addition of this chapter to the book after the original manuscript was completed serves as a metaphor for marriage. Unlike *shanah rishonah*, marriage isn't something that, once you pass a certain point, i.e., twelve months and then it's over, you've made it through, you're done. What has been ingrained in me more than anything else from writing this book, and what I hope you, dear reader, will take away from these pages is that marriage is an ever-transforming, expanding, and dynamic endeavor. It's not something you get good at and then you coast; it's not a book that you finish writing and the story ends. Marriage is dynamic and ever changing, and a good marriage is something you keep working on forever.

My advice: Commit to the process of working on your marriage, enjoy as much of it as you can, and allow your marriage to inspire you to grow into the person and the couple you're meant to be.

———

The chapter that follows is comprised of three distinct sections, all from men who were willing to share their lives and what they've learned over their time being married.

The first section is composed of interviews of men willing to share what they've learned through their experience being married. I chose these specific men to interview because I know them all, and they are all in relationships I respect and admire. I knew they each had a lot of wisdom on the subject of marriage, but the interviews ended up being so much more than I hoped for. Some of the most important ideas this book offers are in the pages you are about to read.

The second section is a parable written by a man who spent much of his life helping couples grow. He counseled couples as a *chesed* because he believed in the importance of marriage. He wrote a parable to illustrate how he saw marriages start and where they eventually went wrong. He used to instruct and educate couples and help them back on the right track to being as happily married as he was *zocheh* to be.

And the third section is a bit of wisdom from my Grandpa, *zt"l*, whom I always admired and felt would want to be part of this book because he believed in marriage, and he knew how to sustain it.

I hope you take the time to read this chapter and enjoy it as much as I have enjoyed putting it together and learning from it. It's not every day you get the opportunity to hear what men have to say on this subject, and believe me, what they have to say is very worth hearing.

●— *Dr. Simcha Shapiro, married 14 years*

Describe marriage in a word.

There are so many words and none of them are sufficient. If I had to choose one word, I would say: "Partnership."

What was the biggest surprise you've experienced in marriage?

Essentially, that someone else can view the world so differently.

And that you married that person?

That part makes sense. When you get married, you are under the influence of all the excitement, but I don't think anyone can anticipate the day-to-day differences and how much they affect day-to-day life. The end of the story is all to our good and all to our betterment, but at the time it feels like it is breaking us, because when you have two separate entities you have to break something in order to make it one. You don't come with a ready-to-go plug and socket that one just plugs into the socket and things work.

We often think, Hey, I was O.K. before, but there are so many areas of our life as single people that aren't equipped to accommodate another person. We're used to making a decision and going with it. There is a certain breaking down that needs to take place in order to make space for another person, for another person's input, and that is a process that starts when you get married and continues once you have children as well.

What stands out in your mind as the biggest adjustment in the first year of marriage?

We all have areas in our lives that we are fastidious about. Often the people we marry don't have the same emphasis. It might be something about food, the way they relate to "things." But the hardest adjustment is communication.

The hardest thing in the first year — wait, the first ten years — of marriage is realizing that just because I said something doesn't mean the other person heard it the way I meant it. How many times have you had a conversation with your spouse when the spouse says, "You didn't say that," and you say, "Yes, I did"? And you realize, sooner or later, that I said it but I didn't say what she thought I said. I'm right that I said it and she's right that I didn't say it. One of the biggest challenges and one of the biggest tikkunim is realizing the difference between what one person says and what another person hears.

When it comes to a marriage, the end question is What should we do? But if you have no understanding of my perspective and I have no understanding of yours, then how can we ever form something that we call "ours"? In every place in my life that I can say, "This is ours," I have helped build our shared spiritual and emotional home. A home and a house is not the same. It's not as easy as signing the mortgage documents.

Building a home happens one brick at a time. Building a home happens every time we have different perspectives on the world and we come to an understanding where we each individually see the world a bit through the perspective of the other person. We come to a place where we accept the validity of the other's perspective, even if we don't agree with it or choose to take on that perspective. And only at that point can we come to a place where we say, "What do we want the perspective of our home to be? What perspective do we want to pass on to our children?"

What do you wish you had known before marriage that would have made things easier or better?

I wish I would have known that many things work themselves out over time. Not to say a couple shouldn't work on their issues, but that some issues do resolve themselves, and in some circumstances you don't always have to "process everything."

I also think having a rav that you both feel comfortable with is hugely important. When things come up, there is a person, a third party, to go to when you need help.

What are the differences between what you imagined marriage to be like and what it is like in reality?

There aren't any. Marriage is what it is. If there is a difference between what I imagined and what marriage is like in reality, then something about my expectations is off. I am very fortunate that my parents have one of the best marriages I have ever seen. Not to say it wasn't hard sometimes, but it was healthy and there were healthy mechanisms about how to deal with things without stuffing them in the closet.

What's something you think every couple should know going into marriage?

Two things. One is marriage is a lot of work, it's really hard work, and to do it right is really hard work. And two, it's the best investment you could possibly make.

What's the best marriage advice you've ever gotten?

It wasn't specifically marriage advice, but it applies to marriage. I believe it's from Steven Covey, who wrote The 7 Habits of Highly Successful People: First seek to understand, then to be understood. Though not given as marriage advice, it's the best advice ever, since 99 percent of disagreements simply dissipate in the face of that advice.

What is one piece of advice you would give a new couple from your own experience?

Once again I'm going to give two pieces of advice. One, be gentle on yourself. It's not easy. It's a huge adjustment. Recognize that any kind of significant change requires adjusting expectations and you need a lot of gentleness with each other and with yourself. And two, pay attention to the feeling of wanting to disengage, of wanting to shut off. Whatever that thing is that makes you feel that way is an opportunity to create closeness or distance. We get to choose.

—————————————• Simcha Gluck, married 13 years

Describe marriage in a word.

Beautiful.

What was the biggest surprise you've experienced in marriage?

How multidimensional it is. There are so many different aspects and so many different things each of us brings to the table. It's a process; it's an amazing process. Working things out together. Choosing to understand each other as opposed to being frustrated by each other. How multidimensional it is on every level.

What stands out in your mind as the biggest adjustment in the first year of marriage?

Realizing that I married someone who is perfect for me, for whom I care deeply, who has so many things that I don't necessarily like, and then having to be O.K. with it. Realizing that you can love someone who can push your buttons and then letting go of your buttons. And also, communication, letting the other person know that there is something to work on a little bit. I think marriage is about letting go of old triggers and at the same time really communicating with the other person from a place of commitment and respect. Finding the balance is what marriage is about.

What do you wish you had known before marriage that would have made things easier or better?

Since it took us twelve years to have our first child, just knowing 100 percent that we were going to have a healthy child someday would have been so helpful to know.

What are the differences between what you imagined marriage to be like and what it is like in reality?

I got married so young that I don't think I had any expectations other than two people who want to become a family.

I think there is more work involved in the reality of it. Life is constantly changing and there is always something to work on. Not only working to stay married but also working to enjoy marriage, working to keep it vibrant and fresh. I think it's important not to underestimate how much work it takes. A big part of that work is getting over ego, and sometimes things don't make sense and you have to be loving anyway. Choosing to agree to get away from drama and focus on a loving relationship.

What's something you think every couple should know going into marriage?

That there is no happily ever after. It's not instant. It's an investment. It is the ultimate investment in time, energy, and resources. But it is so gratifying because you really build something, you build a family. Sometimes there's frustration and upset, but it's about just going back to the root of the commitment and working on getting back there as quickly as possible.

What's the best marriage advice you've ever gotten?

Never focus on being right; always focus on being the right person. It's not about who's right and who's wrong. That is irrelevant. Sometimes you hear people say they married the wrong person, and I think sometimes they are being the wrong person.

What is one piece of advice you would give a new couple from your own experience?

Don't stay in the breakdown, the argument, the fight. When you do that, you don't see the person in any other way. Instead of focusing on the argument, try and get back to empathy and caring as soon as you can. Try and focus on how you can get back to why you love each other.

Any advice for couples having a hard time?

To discern the source of the hard time. Once you decide that you really want to be in this marriage, it's time to go to work. I think that often people don't work out their issues because their ego is too big.

Communication is also really important. You have to make sure you are communicating and sharing what is going on so the other person understands where you are coming from. Give your partner the benefit of the doubt. A lot of the time your partner isn't trying to hurt you but simply comes from a different place and experience and maybe what's going on for one partner and the way she expresses it is very different from the way you are experiencing it or she is experiencing it.

For example, saying good-bye. When one partner doesn't say good-bye, the other partner could feel hurt. Instead of the hurt partner holding back, instead of holding your partner accountable for his or her "sins," if you can express the way it makes you feel, it can open up a conversation and become an opportunity to express yourself and explain where you come from and what you need in the relationship.

———————• *Adam Kenigsberg, married almost 12 years*

Describe marriage in a word.

Teamwork.

What was the biggest surprise you've experienced in marriage?

That a single person could know me so well and thoroughly.

What stands out in your mind as the biggest adjustment in the first year of marriage?

Having to check in with someone to tell her your plans. When you are single, if you're going out, you're going out; you don't have to tell anybody.

What do you wish you had known before marriage that would have made things easier or better?

Pick your battles. Sometimes it's better to let your spouse do what he or she wants rather than fighting over something that ultimately you don't care about all that much.

What are the differences between what you imagined marriage to be like and what it is like in reality?

I don't think I had any preconceived notions. It was just one big blank slate to me. Maybe that's a good thing. Maybe people's expectations get in the way when they hit the reality.

What's something you think every couple should know going into marriage?

If you focus on the needs of your spouse, your needs will be met as a byproduct.

What's the best marriage advice you've ever gotten?

It's a hard one. Did no one give me advice before I got married? Don't try and change your spouse, focus on changing your own character traits.

What is one piece of advice you would give a new couple from your own experience?

Back to what I already said. Focus on the needs of your spouse.

What was the biggest surprise you've experienced in marriage?

That my wife was willing to make aliyah for me.

What stands out in your mind as the biggest adjustment in the first year of marriage?

Living in our own home. Until then I had lived in my parents' home or in yeshivah dorms. Having our own home was totally different. When it's your house, there are a lot of responsibilities that come with it. That took some time for me to adjust to.

What do you wish you had known before marriage that would have made things easier or better?

That my wife could ask me to do something differently than I had been doing it and that I didn't need to take it as a criticism or blow things out of proportion.

What are the differences between what you imagined marriage to be like and what it is like in reality?

I'm a little embarrassed to admit it, but I imagined marriage to be like sheva berachos. Everyone all dressed up, parties, fun, lots of attention. In reality it's a lot of adjustments, flexibility, and the need to be open, to accept the changes Hashem hands you.

What's something you think every couple should know going into marriage?

Failing to plan is planning to fail: Plan things in advance and then be flexible. Life circumstances can change, so it's good to plan what you expect, but you need to also still be flexible.

What's the best marriage advice you've ever gotten?

Don't ever criticize your wife. And try to make your wife your first priority in all aspects of your life.

What is one piece of advice you would give a new couple from your own experience?

Think before you speak. Especially when you're in an intense conversation. Repeat in your head what you want to say three times to make sure you're saying what you truly mean to say.

———————————• Dr. Yonah Amster, married 7½ years

Describe marriage in a word.

Adventure.

What was the biggest surprise you've experienced in marriage?

I can't say I've been overly surprised. I expected lots of surprises so nothing is such a surprise. I've been surprised how nicely it's been going.

What stands out in your mind as the biggest adjustment in the first year of marriage?

Living with someone and all her quirks. Schedule, for example. I wake before 6 a.m. and she wakes up much later. Her nature is to stay up late and sleep in and mine is the opposite.

When we first got married, I was working eighty hours a week in my internship and sleeping over in the hospital every third night, so we had to carve out time to be together, not just spend time together but be really present together. We realized that wasn't working, so I ended up taking a leave of absence to be able to focus on our first year together. I took a job doing research for thirty hours a week and it made a huge difference having that time to spend together. Devoting time to the first year was crucial.

What do you wish you had known before marriage that would have made things easier or better?

That you really need to be well rested. One thing I do before I go home, if I'm feeling tired, is take a fifteen-minute nap. Marriage just goes better when you're rested. That's not to say we are always rested, but life is better when we are. Then when I'm home, I can really be home.

What are the differences between what you imagined marriage to be like and what it is like in reality?

I didn't have that many expectations. I feel like we fight less than I thought we would. When you're dating and engaged, things can be intense. When you settle into marriage and kids, things become less acute; at least that's the way it was for us. When you've settled into life together and you are committed to each other and you're in it for the long haul, it takes a lot of the stress off, and there's no time to fight.

What's something you think every couple should know going into marriage?

Don't have preconceived expectations. Work on yourself. Always think before you speak. Before I say something, I have a three-step process. Step 1: Is what I saw really what I think it is: maybe she didn't do it? Step 2: Maybe she did it but didn't realize it, because she was busy with something else important. Step 3: So what? It can wait. (In other words, I can talk about it later, once it's not bothering me.) Whenever I bring things up right away, it almost always doesn't go well. If I wait, it goes much better.

What's the best marriage advice you've ever gotten?

Not to have too many expectations. You have to be flexible; if something isn't working try something else. And commit yourself to a date night. We go out every Tuesday night. If we miss it, we go out on Friday morning. Even if you don't have a lot of money, that doesn't have to be an issue. You can split a frozen yogurt.

Shanah rishonah is different than when you have kids, but whatever you establish in shanah rishonah will carry on once you have kids. You have to make each other the priority before the kids come. If you didn't, it won't happen after.

What is one piece of advice you would give a new couple from your own experience?

You have to do your research. Constantly re-evaluate what works and what doesn't work. And make tradi-

tions, like going out of town. We go away for two nights twice a year. Once a year we take the kids with us for one night.

Exercise together; go for walks together. I have a saying "a family that works out together, works out." We sit down and have a cup of tea together every night. Family life is until 7:30, and then, when the kids go to bed, our marriage starts. We have tea, we have dinner.

What advice would you give couples that are struggling?

Get help. Make a change. There are always going to be challenges. But you have to be aware enough to know when things are regular challenges and when they are problematic challenges. If you need therapy, get it. If you need to make a move, make it. If the marriage is number one, then everything else can fit around it. You have to make changes so everything else will work around that.

────────● Avraham Greenstein, married 4 years

Describe marriage in a word.

Coordination.

What was the biggest surprise you've experienced in marriage?

How marriage really is what you make it. If you choose to hold yourself to high standards of behavior, that will be the tenor of your marriage, and vice versa. Marriage is not automatically an unavoidable delegation to our basest, most pared-down selves, though it can be. Marriage is an *opportunity to redefine yourself, for better or worse. It is, in any case, a constant and demanding activity.*

What stands out in your mind as the biggest adjustment in the first year of marriage?

My time was no longer my own.

What do you wish you had known before marriage that would have made things easier or better?

The mistakes you make in marriage are hard to undo.

What are the differences between what you imagined marriage to be like and what it is like in reality?

There are more opportunities for closeness than I thought there would be. Marriage doesn't have to be all business, even when you have kids. Small gestures and kind words count for a lot.

What's something you think every couple should know going into marriage?

How to lose a fight gracefully. Also, to know how important it is to have a support system of friends and family who nourish and encourage you individually and as a couple.

What's the best marriage advice you've ever gotten?

Marriage is the opportunity to really do the mitzvah of ahavas Yisrael.

What is one piece of advice you would give a new couple from your own experience?

You don't have to know how to spell marriage to have a good one.

—————————————————● Eran Citrin, married 5 months

Describe marriage in a word.

Bonding.

What was the biggest surprise you've experienced in marriage?

How much time it takes. How much time you need to invest in a new marriage.

What stands out in your mind as the biggest adjustment in your marriage?

Communication. I needed to learn to communicate more. I'm more of a silent type by nature. Learning to communicate deeply was an adjustment. How to share. I needed to share more and that was an adjustment.

Also time. You're used to being alone. So now when someone comes into your life you need to share the time. Especially for me, I work a lot so it's hard. Both having enough time to spend with your spouse and having enough time for yourself.

What do you wish you had known before marriage that would have made things easier or better?

How to plan the wedding better. That would have made for a much easier start to the marriage.

What are the differences between what you imagined marriage to be like and what it is like in reality?

There aren't really any. I haven't been surprised. I was ready to get married and I prepared myself. I knew I needed to do certain things and I did them. Or at least I am trying.

What's something you think every couple should know going into marriage?

That they need to compromise, how to compromise, and on what to compromise. Not on all things but on the important things.

What's the best marriage advice you've ever gotten?

Try to give your wife as much as you can.

What is one piece of advice you would give a new couple from your own experience?

Don't keep things inside. Talk about everything, even if it seems silly. Share everything.

———————• *Ari Abramowitz, married almost 2 months*

Describe marriage in a word.

Good. It was a good-enough description for G-d when He made creation, so I'm going with "good."

What was the biggest surprise you've experienced in marriage?

That it doesn't need to be painful. You can grow and refine your character and your attributes without the fire. It can be just about you wanting to do good for the other, that the growth can be through joy.

Wait, there's something else I want to say. When I come home and there is a pot of mushroom barley soup on the stove, it is so good and so heartwarming. The entire exchange is just warm and loving.

What stands out in your mind as the biggest adjustment in the first year of marriage?

Enjoying going to the grocery store. I used to see the grocery store as something I didn't want to do. It was a chore. But with my wife it's so much fun. Day-to-day things can be so much fun.

What do you wish you had known before marriage that would have made things easier or better?

I wish I'd known I was making the right decision. I knew I was, but I was still scared. Now I realize I should have just calmed down.

What are the differences between what you imagined marriage to be like and what it is like in reality?

I imagined that there would be a lot of fear. I worried that there would be fights and wondered how I would deal with that. In reality, we really enjoy each other. We have a lot of fun doing things together, going places together, and so on. Over all, it's a lot of joy.

What's something you think every couple should know going into marriage?

One piece of advice I received that I find helpful. If there is anything you need to say that is critical it should be a five-to-one ratio, five nice things to one criticism. We've actually set aside a time; every Tuesday evening we sit down and air out whatever we need to talk about. Often by the time Tuesday comes around the issues have resolved themselves. But it's good to take the time to sit down and talk about whatever we need to.

What's the best marriage advice you've ever gotten?

Give the benefit of the doubt. Trust is a very important issue. You need to be able to trust your spouse. And most importantly you need to be careful never to violate that trust. One moment could shatter trust it took months or years to build. So I think trust is of the highest order.

What is one piece of advice you would give a new couple from your own experience?

Be open to finding a relationship coach that can help should you face challenges. I believe that nearly all couples would benefit from investment in their relationship and communication and seeking guidance during the first year, when the foundations are being laid. This can prevent much heartache and pain. That is one piece. Having a date night is the other.

Describe marriage in a word.

Shleimus. It doesn't translate well in a western context, but that's the word. Shleimus.

What was the biggest surprise you've experienced in marriage?

That it worked out. Yeah, that it worked.

What stands out in your mind as the biggest adjustment in the first year of marriage?

To stop thinking about myself, my own needs.

What do you wish you had known before marriage that would have made things easier or better?

Nothing; that's part of the fun of marriage, that things work out.

What are the differences between what you imagined marriage to be like and what it's like in reality?

I thought it would be a lot worse. I was pleasantly surprised to find that it's really terrific.

What's something you think every couple should know going into marriage?

Compromise. When I wash my face in the bathroom, I'm very liberal with the water, and I get it all over. My wife doesn't want to walk on a wet bathroom floor. So we compromised. After I wash my face, I put down a towel. She didn't have to change and I didn't have to change. A good win/win is when everyone comes out feeling like they won.

Here's another one: Right now we live in a small apartment. It's so small that if my wife wants to talk on the phone while I'm sleeping, it will wake me. For a while I said, "Lower your voice, lower your voice," but it wasn't working, so we worked out a compromise that if I'm sleeping and my wife wants to talk on the phone she walks outside. She's happy and gets a walk and I'm happy too.

Another example is when we were first married, my wife would make dinner and then ask me, "How do you like it?" The first time I didn't like something I said, "It's terrible." Well, that was a big mistake. She cried and it wasn't good. So eventually we made a compromise. If I didn't like something, she said it was fine to tell her but I should wait a couple of days. And that has worked for us ever since.

What's the best marriage advice you've ever gotten?

Before I got married, Rav Moshe Eisemann, mashgiach of Ner Yisrael, told me never to make Torah an excuse. If your wife asks you to take out the garbage, don't say, "I was just sitting down to learn." Help your wife.

What is one piece of advice you would give a new couple from your own experience?

I told you, compromise!

The Parable of the Garden

by David Hyman, *zt"l*
edited by Ruth Hyman

Long ago, in an imaginary tale, a young man and woman were introduced. They dated and soon realized their destiny was to be together forever. They wanted to marry. The young man planned that they would visit her father to seek his blessing. The couple traveled out to the country, where the girl's widowed father lived alone in a small cottage, surrounded by a stone wall.

As he slowly opened the door, the old man saw the glow on his daughter's face and the earnest, determined look in the young man's eyes. The couple stood in the doorway, and the old man immediately understood the situation. He smiled and beckoned them into his humble home. The young man was struck by the simplicity of the furnishings, the small painting of the girl's mother on the mantel over the fireplace, and the quaint, handmade tablecloth covering a wooden table. The three of them sat on old, sturdy chairs around the table.

The young woman spoke to her father about her intended, the dreams they shared of the future. Misty eyed, the old man savored her words like beautiful music, his wrinkled face smiling with approval as she spoke. He looked at the young man, who reminded him of himself many years before. When she finished, she glanced down and then at the young man, who began to speak. He told of his desire to care for the man's daughter, to marry her, and to build a bayis ne'eman b'Yisrael.

The old man looked pleased and grasped their hands in his. "Of course I give you my blessing," he said tearfully. "And there is something else I want to give you. After my daughter, it is the most precious thing I have since my *wife passed away." He stood up slowly and motioned to the back door. The young couple followed the man, whose aging gait was slow but steady.*

Opening the door, a magnificent garden was revealed in full bloom. "This is my gift to you both," said the girl's father, stepping onto the walkway. "My wife and I planted this garden together many years ago. You two look around while I catch my breath — I am so overwhelmed with joy." Near the entrance to the garden, he sat down on a rustic bench beneath a tree, whose limbs were bent with ripened fruit.

Together the young couple explored the garden. A winding dirt path lined with smooth, white stones led through the perfectly maintained lawn, where every blade was uniformly cut. The array of flowers and bushes was like a visual symphony, bursting forth in color, and all of the beds were meticulously free of weeds. There were shade trees and trees bearing beautiful fruit. Birds sang, adding yet another dimension to the scene.

High above the garden, billowy white clouds hung beneath a blue sky and the sun poured its warmth over everything. To the young man, it was beauty beyond anything he'd ever seen. And, for the young woman, it reminded her of the idyllic life she'd known as a little girl and one she hoped to build with her future husband. She recalled how her father and mother lovingly labored in the garden together, side by side.

In springtime, her parents ritually dug up the old, dying plants and replaced them with new ones. They continually weeded the flowerbeds together and pruned the trees. She recalled that when she was a girl, summertime was spent enjoying the fruit from the trees and playing hide-and-seek. On warm summer days, the three of them would picnic on the lawn and savor the garden's bounty.

Every fall, her father weeded and her mother planted bulbs for the coming year. Against the stone wall, a small wood shed in the corner of the garden contained a potting table and an array of old, well-cared-for garden tools. Moss covered the roof and the glass panes in the door allowed sunlight to bathe the interior.

The young couple walked back to the old man, sitting peacefully on the bench. Believing that his daughter's future and the future of his precious garden were secure, he had gently passed away in his sleep. Sad though she was to lose her father, the young woman realized that he had lived a full life and she took solace that he had rejoined her mother in the next world.

The young couple married later that summer, and moved into the cottage where the love between them began to grow. At first, they enjoyed spending time in the garden, although they did little to maintain it. The flowers were magnificent, the grass still green and the trees hung low with fruit. As summer turned to fall, they spent less time outside. The newlyweds were attracted to the village nearby, with its cozy inn, delicious food and drink, and many new friends.

Darkness came early in the chilly autumn evenings, and they hardly noticed the fallen leaves covering the lawn or the unpicked fruit now rotting on the ground. As the days grew shorter, the blue skies turned gray, flowers wilted and died, and the grass grew wild. Inside the cozy cottage, the newlyweds warmed themselves by the stone fireplace. The old man had cut and stored enough firewood to last several winters.

The young couple looked forward to springtime when they could once again enjoy the beauty of the outdoors and the mystical garden. As the days began to lengthen, they looked out and realized how much work was needed to restore what they had neglected. One early spring day, they ventured out, and the young man tried to open the door of the shed. It broke off the hinges, and he promised himself that he would repair it later. They found the tools, which had become a bit rusty, and carried them into the garden.

He started to rake the leaves and she began weeding the flowerbeds. They spoke lovingly to each other, and she began to hum a tune that she remembered from her childhood. At first, they enjoyed working together in the garden, although there was much to do. When he broke the rake, the young man said something harsh, which surprised the young woman. As she worked in the soil, her hands became dirty and she worried they might not get clean.

The warmth of the early spring day soon turned cool as the sun began its descent. Friends stopped by on their way to the village and bid them to come along. The young couple welcomed the opportunity to leave their work and left their tools in the garden — hurrying to freshen up and join the fun.

The days turned into weeks, months, and years of neglect that took their toll on the garden and on the young couple. The once-lovely place of tranquility and joy became less and less so. It became nearly impossible to walk along the dirt path that was now covered with weeds. The white stones were strewn about and vines engulfed the little shed. As the garden became overgrown, the couple became overwhelmed. They eventually ran out of firewood and were cold. "Once upon a time" wasn't going quite the way they had expected and the two of them began to wonder if they could get back on the path to "happily ever after."

Epilogue

David, z"l, was devoted to helping couples grow their marriages to greatness. He built his expertise in marriage using ours as a testing ground. We lived in the marriage laboratory! He read extensively on the topic, sought out mentors, and, most importantly, put what he learned into practice. One of his great joys was sharing his thoughts on marriage with newly engaged couples. He believed a great marriage was attainable if the couple was just willing to put in the effort as anything worthwhile in life takes hard work. He wrote "The Parable of the Garden" to make this point.

Marriage tips from David, z"l:

- *Care about your marriage.*

- *Don't settle for "just O.K."*

- *Learn what makes each of you happy.*

- *Use good manners.*

- *Learn to communicate effectively.*

- *Treat your marriage as a priority.*

And Ruth:

- *If he treats her like a queen, she will make him her king.*

- *Use good manners; treat each other at least as well as you would treat a stranger — or your boss*

- *We learn in Melachim I 6:7, "Hammers, chisels, or any iron utensils were not heard in the Temple when it was being built." Likewise, as we build our mikdashei me'at, we should avoid the "iron" of harsh speech.*

- *Make it real, work to do what makes each other happy.*

- *Banish complacency.*

Advice From My Grandpa, Warren H. Frank

My grandparents met when my grandmother was still a teenager and my grandpa was twenty. The first time they met, my grandfather knew he was going to marry her, but she was too young. Years passed, he went off to war, survived, came home and they got married. They had four children together and cared for each other intensely until the day he passed away in his eighties. They were married for almost sixty years, and it was clear just from looking at each other how much they cared for each other.

I grew up watching them, seeing how two completely different people could build a life together and be truly happy together for nearly sixty years. I always admired them, their commitment to one another, their desire to make the other happy and take care of the other. Watching them was watching a marriage work. Not because it was hard work, but because they understood each other so well they made it look easy.

At the end of my grandfather's life, he was very challenged. He lost his sight rapidly, which was extremely devastating for him. A few years later he was told he had a terminal disease. My grandmother took care of him like a professional caregiver. Not so differently from how she had taken care of him their whole life together, just more intensely. Even when my grandfather couldn't see, he told my grandmother she looked beautiful every day. They were an inspirational couple and I always felt honored to watch them together. Relationships like theirs were such a rare commodity I wanted to learn everything I could and replicate it if I was zocheh to such a marriage.

I wanted to share some of my grandpa's wisdom with you in this section. Here are a few thoughts from my pater-

nal grandfather, Warren H. Frank, zichrono levrachah, as told in his voice:

"You have to understand who the other person is and adapt. Allow the other person to be who he really is. You're not going to change him so embrace him.

"Gramma always takes a long time to get ready to go out for the night. I don't. So I account for that. I know after I am ready to go I should pull out the newspaper or a book because I am going to have a long wait. You adjust for the other person. You take care of him. You make it work. She takes care of me, and I take care of her. That's the secret to a long and loving marriage. You have to let go of the things that don't matter, be honest with who you are and what you need and who the other person is and what she needs, and make it work.

"Marriage is like life. You have to keep wiggling."

What does that mean?

"You have to keep trying, keep moving, you know — wiggling. Something doesn't go right. You keep wiggling, keep working on it, keep thinking about it, you wiggle and you wiggle till things fall into place or you get them into place. You keep trying. You try and you try and you make it work!"

Part 3

Let's Talk About It...

Chapter 13

Tips and Tricks on Running a Home

When I thought about getting married, my mind was filled with thoughts of decorating an apartment. I envisioned myself walking down the aisles of my favorite department store, buying everything and anything I wanted to decorate my new home. I was excited and felt like I had waited so long to create my own home, I never gave a moment's thought to how I was going to keep my new home looking sparkling and guest ready.

When I finally got to my first apartment with my new husband, we realized there was a lot more to keeping a home than a color scheme and curtains. Though I thought I was a neat person and fairly organized, I didn't realize what it was like to keep house until I got married. I found it very difficult to merge my style with my husband's, and, at times, I felt overwhelmed and frustrated. Neither of us was experienced in what we were doing, since we both had only lived in our parents' homes or dorms. My grandmother always made it look so easy, but I soon realized there was a lot more to it than she let on. Keeping house and turning it into a home is an art and a skill. The sooner you learn it, the easier and more enjoyable your life and home will be.

It's different when you're married and living in your own home and not in a dorm or your parents' home. Not only do you have to figure out your own style, but you also have to learn your husband's. With this in mind, I'm offering some tips and tricks to make your life easier and your home a cleaner, neater place to invite guests and unexpected drop-in relatives.

Be Prepared

The main idea I want to impart is to *stay on top of things* and don't let them build up. So often we feel we are too busy to put things away or wash the dinner dishes, but it's easy to forget how much more stress is caused by needing to do twice as much the next day. A clean home also creates a calm environment where it is easier to think clearly and be productive.

Before I restructured my perspective, I used to try to clean, shop, and cook on Friday for Shabbos. Then I realized that if you stay on top of the house all week, there's no need to clean on Friday at all. Now I spend five minutes on Fridays sweeping and putting away any last-minute things and my cleaning is done.

I also make it a point to try to do laundry each time a load is ready, so I don't need a whole day for laundry. My grandmother, she should live and be well, always put a load of laundry in the washer before she went to bed and then simply added soap and turned it on in the morning. If you are going to be at work, it may be best to turn it on when you walk in the door after work so you can finish the load and put it away before you go to bed. I find the load-of-laundry-a-day habit very helpful.

Food preparation is another area where preparing ahead makes all the difference. On Sunday, I make a menu for the week and shop with my menu in mind.

These may seem like simple ideas, but staying on top of your home will help you feel capable and confident and never worry if your husband brings his *chavrusa* home unexpectedly or your in-laws call to let you know they will be coming over in half an hour.

Another important idea to remember is that it's all right to ask for help. I know you are newly married and want to treat your husband like the king he is, but you have to remember that you are also a queen and queens know how to delegate. Either ask your husband for help or, if he isn't interested or can't do it and you have the resources, consider hiring someone on occasion.

Remember that this is just the beginning. Though it is fun to "play house" now and take on all these new roles — super chef, housekeeper, helpmate, and working woman — before long, G-d willing, it won't be just the two of you. There will come a day when you will need some extra support. The better habits you develop now, the easier life will be in the future.

The day you come home from the hospital with a new baby is not the time to start teaching your husband how to make soup or do the laundry. Consider having a conversation about how you each envision dividing the household responsibilities, which jobs you'd each like to take on, and which jobs you both hate and either have to divide or hire someone to do.

Each couple has to find what works for them. I have a friend whose husband does all the cooking. She washes the floor, does the ironing, and works full-time. In our family, we have divided the housekeeping into some fairly stereotypical categories. I cook and my husband takes care of the banking and makes sure the bills are paid on time. He takes out the garbage, and I fold and put away the clothes. We both try to help each other by putting in a load of laundry. These are divisions that work for us, and we feel good about them. We have each taken our talents — his head for math and my flair in the kitchen — and found a niche for ourselves.

Also keep in mind that life changes. Just because you designated certain chores to each other in the beginning of your marriage doesn't mean they have to be your roles forever. You can experiment and change jobs whenever you want. The goal is to find a system that works for you as a couple.

Keep a Schedule

Learn to schedule. Get a day planner that fits in your purse. Start writing things down. When I was learning how to keep house, I would schedule each task so I knew what I had to do each day.

Sample Schedule:

- *Sunday:* Plan menus for the week, shop for groceries, wash and put away laundry, wash floors, cook dinner with leftovers. (We like leftovers; not everyone does.)

- *Monday:* Clean bathrooms, sweep floors, make dinner.

- *Tuesday:* Wash floors, do laundry.

- *Wednesday:* Pick one area and declutter for twenty minutes, shop for Shabbos.

- *Thursday:* Buy last-minute items for Shabbos, cook Shabbos meals or part of them.

- *Friday:* Straighten up, finish last-minute items, wash floors, set Shabbos table.

- *Motza'ei Shabbos*: Wash dishes, get house back in shape.

Each couple's list will look different. That was just an example, but the most important thing I can offer you is to keep up your home daily. My grandmother told me she never went to bed without putting the house in order. That way, when she woke up the next morning her head was clear. She could accomplish her goals for the day instead of having to take time to tidy up from the day before.

I can't say I have never gone to bed without the house in perfect shape, especially since our kids have been born. But I can honestly say that I try to stay on top of things every day. Each time I leave a room, I look to see what is out of place and try to restore the room to order. When you are involved with keeping things neat, it takes only a minute a few times a day, as opposed to what I remember from my high school years. Then I would need all of Sunday to clean my room and do my laundry because I had let it go all week.

Once you get the hang of this system, you'll see how much calmer and happier your home and family will be. *Baruch Hashem*, I now have two boys ages six and three and a new baby girl. The boys love to follow me around and help me clean. I have taught them that when we clean our home, we are making it a dwelling place for Hashem's *Shechinah*, like the Beis HaMikdash. They are little *kohanim*, so they relate to that example. Once in a while, I will catch them cleaning up or sweeping with their little broom. If I ask what they are doing, they will say something like, "I am cleaning up because I want Hashem to come over."

In my humble opinion, life has enough chaos in it without your house contributing to it. If you can create a calm, clean, and stable home, it offers a safe haven from the outside world. It can also provide inner peace and calm to you and your family that is invaluable.

More Tips and Tricks

- Clearly define jobs and chores.

- Stay on top of things.

- Do twenty minutes of decluttering at least once a week: clean out a closet, organize a shelf, throw out old papers, and so on.

- Take five minutes every day to put each room back in order before you go to sleep.

- Don't let dishes build up in the sink. Wash dishes as you use them. Scour your sink at least once a week. My grandmother did hers daily. If your sink is clean, it will make the rest of the kitchen follow. I didn't make up this idea, but I know it to be true.

- Pick one day a month to do deep cleaning, like moving furniture and sweeping behind it.

- Pick a consistent day each week to wash sheets and blankets.

- Do your meal planning before you go shopping. Don't go grocery shopping hungry!

- Keep to-do lists. They make life much easier, and it feels great to check things off as you complete them.

- Realize that keeping your home clean, neat, and organized isn't a chore; it is an honor. Hashem is giving you a home to take care of. Look at the attention you focus on keeping your home running as your *avodas Hashem*.

These suggestions are just a few to get you going. If you find they are helpful and want more guidance in this area of your life, I highly suggest researching techniques and resources for home organization and cleaning. There are great ideas easily available. The difference they will make in your day-to-day life can be fantastic.

Conclusion

So Shanah Rishonah Is Over — Where Do We Go from Here?

If by now you are at the end of your *shanah rishonah*, mazel tov! I'm sure you've grown a lot and made huge strides in your personal development as well as grown as a couple. Hopefully this year has been filled with wonder and discovery and lots of fun. Hopefully you've gotten to know yourself and your spouse a lot better over the past year. My wish is that this book has given you some resources and tools that helped enhance that process.

Moving into your second year is like the end of *sheva berachos. Now what are we going to do with ourselves?* you might ask. Don't think the ideas and stories in this book are only meant to inspire a successful *shanah rishonah*. Marriage is a process that deepens and grows with time. I would like you to think of the advice in this book as a gift you can take with you into future years and stages of your marriage.

Look back at these pages whenever you feel like you could use some support or don't want to feel alone in your experience. In compiling this book, I found it gratifying and helpful to read stories that describe parts of my relationship and see that it isn't only us.

As I was finishing this book, I was particularly amused and comforted by Beth Shapiro's story, "Expecting in *Shanah Rishonah*." I called my husband into the room and said, "See, I'm not crazy. It's not just me." It turns out Beth and I have similar experiences when we are expecting. After almost ten years of marriage and expecting my third child, I found comfort in knowing that I am not alone.

The rest of your marriage is ahead of you. Make the best of each moment, cherish each other, and remember how much we all have to be grateful for. The best is yet to come.

Appendix

Mishegas or Mental Illness?

When I was a little girl visiting my grandmother in Florida, I remember she and my mother having a discussion over coffee.

"It's his *mishegas*," one said to the other. "Why are you making such a big deal?"

To this day I don't remember the rest of the conversation, but the idea that everyone has their *mishegas* certainly stuck with me. I remember other childhood moments when the term *mishegas* was used.

Mishegas was used playfully when my other grandmother, she should live and be well, couldn't sit down and enjoy her dinner until she had cleaned up all the dinner dishes. *Mishegas* was the term used when an aunt made a bar mitzvah that felt more like a royal wedding in England. And *mishegas* was the term used when a friend's new husband insisted on emptying the garbage cans in the house when they reached half full. The idea of a full or, G-d forbid, overflowing garbage made him cringe.

Everyone has some sort of *mishegas* or another. *Mishegas* isn't considered bad. These quirks make us individuals and sometimes make the people around us have to strive a little harder to love everything about us. In marriage, the chance of finding out a little bit about your own *mishegas* and your spouse's is inevitable.

A question arises, not when a person has a *mishegas*, but when the *mishegas* affects his or her life to the point of interfering with normal functioning. Quirks are one thing, but being dysfunctional from a seeming *mishegas* is where a line sometimes needs to be drawn to distinguish when a mental illness is at play and needs attention and treatment.

Finding that your spouse has a mental challenge doesn't have to be a divorce sentence, G-d forbid. However, the stress put on a marriage by a mental illness can be very challenging and lead to divorce without proper help and support. The best thing to do when you learn there are mental or emotional challenges in yourself or your partner is to get the best help possible as soon as possible. This is especially true when the condition wasn't identified before marriage or intensified with the stress of marriage. In most cases, before you can decide what you are going to do about the situation, you have to learn about it to know what you're dealing with.

The following information is designed to help you understand the spectrum of mental illness, what can be done about it, and how it can be addressed in a marriage. It is meant to help you begin the process of understanding mental illnesses and if it is affecting your life. If it is, you may want to consider seeking advice from a professional mental health practitioner.

The most important thing a person dealing with or married to a person with a mental challenge can do is to take action and get help. You should consult with a knowledgeable and experienced Rabbi or Rebbetzin — or with a recognized referral agency — to find the proper therapist for the issues confronting you.

The world of mental illness is an ever-expanding and changing science. The following information does not constitute a diagnosis and cannot substitute for seeking a professional in the mental health care field. They are merely explanations to help one begin to ask the questions that may eventually lead to a happier, healthier life for all those involved.

Hatzlachah. May you be guided by Hashem on the journey toward health.

Red Flags of Mental Illness

● Dr. Lindsay Jordan, Psychiatrist

S*hanah rishonah* can be quite exhilarating, but also quite challenging. It is a time of discovering who you are, who your spouse is, and how you will both mesh together. One may feel as if one is on a roller coaster of soaring thrills and downward disappointments as one adjusts to the reality and complexities of married life.

Ideally, a couple will learn to appreciate each other's strengths and weaknesses. Ample patience may be needed to give both partners the necessary time and space to grow. Communicating openly about your feelings, desires, and needs can greatly facilitate things. A spouse may be very willing to work on himself if the information is conveyed in a warm, sensitive, and supportive manner. It is important to keep in mind that people can and do make great personal changes, but most behavioral changes occur in small increments over long periods of time, with lots of fits and starts. You will be surprised how much you will both mature as the years pass!

The Effects of Stress on Mental Health

A minority of couples will stumble across more significant issues that go beyond differences in personality and modes of operating. We all have certain emotional vulnerabilities that may become more accentuated in times of stress. For example, many people react to a week of poor sleep with irritability, poor concentration, headaches, and impaired judgment. Experiencing a significant loss, such as the death of a loved one, can result in feelings of shock, anger, and guilt. The sadness and pain can necessitate a long process of healing. Sometimes a person may feel unable to adjust to a particular stressor, such as significant financial loss.

In such cases, short-term counseling from an experienced counselor may ease the adjustment disorder. It can be beneficial to have extra support and an outside perspective beyond that of friends and family. With time and much effort, a couple can find ways to buttress each other during stressful times and to compensate for each other's weaknesses.

Some people with biological and psychological vulnerabilities will react to stressors with more significant emotional distress. A person's genetic inheritance may predispose a person to cope poorly in the face of emotional challenges. The person's psychological makeup and possible childhood traumas can further contribute to reduced resiliency.

Such vulnerabilities are often not known prior to marriage, as the onset of mental health problems may not occur until the twenties or thirties, or they may not have materialized until the person was faced with adult responsibilities. Other times, the person has struggled to some degree with mental health issues prior to marriage, but the issues were minimized or compensated for by the family.

It can be very hard for a new spouse to adjust to such issues when they arise unexpectedly without advanced preparation. Learning about mental health can help a couple support each other through hard times. People struggling with emotional challenges often react in telltale ways, and knowing these signs can help loved ones know when professional help is needed. Not being able to get out of bed due to lack of energy and motivation may indicate that depression is brewing.

People struggling with anxiety may be unable to deal with normal daily events and obligations. Emotional symptoms can be disabling, overwhelming, and unbearably painful. Much time and energy may be spent just coping with symptoms. School, work, relationships, and childrearing may get neglected. In response to one's poor functioning, a person may then experience fear, embarrassment, loneliness, and a sense of worthlessness.

Reductions in stress can have a big impact on relieving emotional distress. A spouse who provides a sense of security and understanding can alleviate some of the sufferer's burden. Addressing emotional issues early and with appropriate professional care can lead toward prompt resolution and prevent the formation of more chronic problems.

Emotional and behavioral problems become known as a mental disorder when symptoms impair one's functioning in various parts of one's life. It is useful to know basic descriptions of the various common mental health conditions, so as to know when professional help is needed. Recognizing that marital conflicts may stem from a mental health condition enables one to acquire appropriate help and to have more empathy.

People with mental health issues can be quite irritable and even difficult. The couple may find themselves arguing extensively or feeling very distant. It may be hard to overlook the frequent negative encounters in order to focus on the big picture; namely, that one's spouse is suffering with mental health issues. With appropriate treatment, however, most people with mental health conditions will go on to live meaningful and happy lives. Much effort may be required, but the potential for a loving and healthy marriage still exists.

Anxiety Disorders

According to the National Institute of Mental Health, based on 2005 data, 26 percent of the United States adult population is diagnosable in a given year for one or more mental disorders. A variety of anxiety disorders collectively make up the most common mental disorders that Americans experience. Less prevalent but still significant are disorders of mood, personality, and attention. Finally, 6 percent of American adults experience severe mental illness requiring more intensive and chronic treatment. This includes major depressive disorder, bipolar disorder, and schizophrenia, and they typically do not manifest until one's twenties or thirties. For the vast majority of mental health conditions, valuable treatments are available and improvement will occur.

The average age of onset for all disorders combined is fourteen years old, which means that many anxiety disorders start in childhood. Although everyone feels intense anxiety during certain stressful periods, having a disorder implies that one's sense of fear or danger does not fit the situation and is impairing one's ability to go about daily life tasks.

Postpartum conditions, which are rooted in one's biological state, influence one's emotional state and can lead to a wide spectrum of mental health conditions, including anxiety. It's well known that many women experience postpartum blues or mild mood swings after childbirth. The change in hormones and sleep deprivation may lead to feeling exhausted, anxious, and weepy. Many women will also experience moodiness, sadness, difficulty sleeping, irritability, appetite changes, or concentration problems. These symptoms will typically dissipate after several days to a couple of weeks.

For some women with a genetic predisposition, childbirth may elicit a more serious and longer-lasting condition called *postpartum depression*. The symptoms of postpartum depression include a lack of energy and motivation, feelings of worthlessness and guilt, changes in appetite, changes in sleep, and general loss of interest in life. Other signs include lack of interest in the baby, negative feelings toward the baby, worrying about hurting the baby, and lack of concern for one-self. The mother may even develop recurrent thoughts of death or suicide. Postpartum depression often starts soon after child-birth and develops gradually over months, but it can come on suddenly, sometimes several months after giving birth.

A woman who experiences postpartum depression should receive immediate professional help. A combination of appropriate supports, medication, and therapy will enable a woman to recover and resume caring for her family. Early recognition is vital, and family members should provide much-needed empathy and help with reducing stress.

Phobias, the most prevalent of the anxiety disorders, involves persistent fear and avoidance of a specific object or situation, such as spiders, heights, and flying.

Social anxiety disorder engenders intense panic during social situations and when talking to new people or in large groups. The intense fear of being judged and the feelings of embarrassment and humiliation may inhibit one from even leaving one's house. One's marital relationship may be impacted by the curtailment of social activities.

Constant, exaggerated fearfulness or nervousness characterizes **generalized anxiety disorder**. A person becomes consumed by constant worries about everyday problems and has associated physical ailments such as trembling, heart palpitations, sweating, headaches, and stomachaches. Although a person realizes that his anxiety is more intense than the situation warrants, he cannot calm his concerns. As they anticipate problems with their finances, health, and relationships, the tension in the house rises precipitously.

People with a **panic disorder** have repetitive sudden episodes of intense fear along with an impending sense of doom. The attacks include terrifying physical sensations such as chest pain, heart palpitations, shortness of breath, dizziness, and abdominal distress. Treatment involves learning and practicing behavioral techniques that reduce anxiety. Various medications can also reduce the intensity of the anxiety. Lifestyle changes will also reduce inner tension.

Post-traumatic stress disorder (PTSD) develops in some people who experience sudden or ongoing trauma. PTSD can result from physical or emotional abuse, accidents, war experiences, and natural or human-caused disasters. The traumatic events are painfully relived through intrusive recollections. Anything triggering a memory of the trauma is adamantly avoided.

Other manifestations of PTSD include irritability, sleep problems, numb feelings, and startling easily. A person with PTSD may struggle in a relationship due to feelings of emotional detachment, impaired coping, and intense anger at times. Cognitive behavioral therapy (discussed below) is the mainstay of treatment for PTSD. Judicial use of medications will also provide relief.

Finally, ***obsessive-compulsive disorder*** (OCD) causes one to obsess over unwanted and irrational thoughts. In response to these intrusive thoughts, the person is compelled to perform repetitive behaviors to reduce the resultant anxiety. Common obsessive themes involve fears of contamination, ordering and checking things, and hoarding things. Compulsive acts may involve excessive hand washing, praying, counting, or intense guilt.

Without appropriate medication, along with a therapy called *"**exposure and response prevention**,"* the person with OCD is unable to stop these thoughts and ritualized behaviors. There is little time left over for daily activities, responsibilities, or engaging emotionally with one's partner. In the *frum* community, OCD can sometimes take the form of overly scrupulous observance of mitzvos, so that the person is no longer serving Hashem but rather their biologically induced aberrant thinking.

Attention Disorders

It is awe inspiring to ponder the intricate design of our brains and to realize how slight alterations in our chemical makeup can impact our thoughts, attention, and concentration. Nine percent of United States children aged thirteen to eighteen have *attention deficit hyperactivity disorder* (ADHD). The prevalence of ADHD in U.S. adults is lower — 4 percent — since many will have strengthened their areas of weakness as children.

In adults, ADHD symptoms include difficulty paying attention to boring tasks, such as paying bills. A person with ADHD may find it impossible to get organized, stick to a task, or remember appointments. Daily tasks such as performing housework efficiently, arriving at work on time, and being productive on the job can be quite challenging.

ADHD may affect a person's ability to get motivated and organized for complex tasks, such as taking a higher-education class. It may lead him to being more reckless and having more traffic accidents. Adults with ADHD may be quite restless and may attempt to do several things at once, most of them unsuccessfully. They tend to prefer "quick fixes" rather than slowly taking the steps needed to achieve greater rewards.

The greatest impact on relationships often revolves around the person's emotional reactivity and quick temper. Daily exercise can greatly improve concentration and restlessness, as will a healthy diet and adequate sleep. Other crucial treatments involve appropriate medications, supportive counseling, and learning compensatory strategies such as using a daily planner.

People with ADHD can be quite frustrating to live with, but their inherent weaknesses can be transformed into great strengths of impulsive creativity and energetic productivity. Many successful people harness their ADHD traits to become greater thinkers, entrepreneurs, artists, and *chesed* activists.

Substance Abuse

People can become addicted to many things, including the Internet, gambling, alcohol, and, of course, drugs. Essentially, *addiction* involves the compulsive use of something despite incurring negative consequences. Neglecting responsibilities and abandoning favorite pastimes may be the first sign of abuse. Other signals include decreased work performance, financial problems, secretiveness, changes in friends and routine, and frequently getting into legal trouble. Abuse of drugs may cause changes in appetite or sleep patterns, deterioration of personal grooming habits, unusual smells, bloodshot eyes, tremors, slurred speech, or impaired coordination. People who abuse drugs and alcohol often waste away their talents and opportunities as their lives become more and more chaotic.

Physical dependence involves the development of tolerance to the drug's effects, taking drugs to avoid withdrawal symptoms, using more drugs than intended, and spending excessive time on obtaining and using drugs. With repeated use, abused substances alter the way the brain looks and functions. The brains of people with substance dependence are biologically primed to continue using drugs despite the accrual of many life problems. These changes interfere with the ability to think clearly, have good judgment, control one's behavior, and feel good without drugs.

People with substance abuse problems may also develop blackouts, infections, mood swings, depression, and paranoia. Drug use can cause personality changes, angry outbursts, agitation, lethargy, and anxiety.

Overcoming drug addiction is possible, but it requires recognition, commitment, and tremendous effort. Twelve-step programs have proven highly effective in guiding people toward recovery. There are *frum* twelve-step programs that can support a religious person on the path to recovery. Various medications can also help people overcome cravings for some substances.

Many people will benefit from substance abuse treatment clinics that provide necessary support and therapy. The Jewish community has developed substance abuse programs that cater to our unique needs. The nonaddicted spouse may benefit from specially designed therapies as well.

Making lifestyle changes that address the root cause of the addiction will be critical. Although addiction places great strain on a marriage and requires much support and intervention, it is possible for a couple to weather this challenge together.

Mood Disorders

Sometimes, a couple may have to contend with one or both partners having a mood disorder. Around 10 percent of American adults have mood disorders, consisting mostly of major depressive disorder and bipolar disorder.

Although everyone has occasional periods of feeling sad, a person with *major depressive disorder* experiences a severely depressed mood and activity level that persists for two or more weeks. The depression impacts one's appetite, sleep, energy level, and concentration. One feels entirely hopeless and may experience irrational guilt and feelings of worthlessness. Thoughts of self-harm and suicide may take hold.

Symptoms significantly interfere with daily functioning, and relationships are impacted by the person's inability to be emotionally and physically present. Such clinical depression necessitates a multifaceted treatment plan that includes medication, therapy, and relief of stress.

Bipolar disorder is characterized by dramatic shifts in mood, energy, and activity levels that affect a person's ability to carry out daily tasks. These biologically induced shifts in mood and energy levels are more extreme than the typical highs and lows experienced by most of us. People with bipolar disorder experience repeated episodes of depression and mania.

A person experiencing mania feels unusually "high," optimistic, or extremely irritable. This biologically induced mood state engenders unrealistic beliefs about one's powers and creates a sense of heightened invincibility, creativity, and euphoria. A person with mania talks rapidly, has racing thoughts, functions on little sleep, and has excess energy. Mania feels good, but the person often spirals out of control with reckless spending, foolish investments, and impulsive behavior. Mania also presents as anger and aggression, with the person picking fights, lashing out needlessly, and blaming others who criticize their irrational behavior.

Bipolar disorder requires treatment with mood-stabilizing medications as well as supportive therapy. Establishing regular daily schedules with a fixed sleep pattern can also help stabilize the mood.

Personality Disorders

Some people have ingrained patterns of behavior and interpersonal interactions that make relationships with them extremely challenging.

Personality disorders exist in 9 percent of American adults and represent fixed patterns of relating to others that markedly affect daily life in a negative way. *Avoidant personality disorder* is characterized by extreme social inhibition, feelings of inadequacy, and excess sensitivity to rejection. People with avoidant personality disorder feel extremely insecure and refrain from most social interactions, thereby greatly inhibiting their life experiences.

People who have *borderline personality disorder* struggle to regulate their emotions and thoughts. The disorder leads to impulsive and reckless behavior, as well as unstable relationships with others. People with this disorder tend to alternate between intense idealization and intense hatred of loved ones.

Other disorders, such as depression, anxiety, substance abuse, and eating disorders, often coexist with borderline personality disorder. Self-harm, suicidal behaviors, and suicide may also occur.

Antisocial personality disorder involves a consistent disregard for the rights of others. Such people disregard social norms and laws. They repeatedly lie, place others at risk for their own benefit, and lack remorse for their offenses. Relationships with such people often entail repeated betrayal and victimization.

Treatment for personality disorders involves long-term therapy. Through concerted effort at practicing more functional ways of interacting, people with this disorder can smooth out their rough edges and develop mutually satisfying relationships.

Finally, *schizophrenia* is a rarely occurring, chronic mental illness. It is characterized by deficits in thought processes, perceptions, and emotional responsiveness. People with schizophrenia experience delusions, disorganized thoughts, and hallucinations. The disorder also causes a lack of motivation to accomplish goals, difficulties with engaging in social interactions, and emotional blunting. These symptoms make holding a job, forming relationships, and other day-to-day functions especially difficult. Medications, enhanced supports, and rehabilitation programs are the mainstay of treatment for schizophrenia.

Treatments

Thankfully, there are many effective treatments available that have been scientifically validated. It is important to find qualified professionals who can work with one's life situation and value system.

When first encountering mental health symptoms, a visit to the primary-care physician is necessary to rule out physical health problems as an underlying cause. However, major crises involving the potential for harm to self or others would indicate an immediate evaluation in the emergency room.

Symptoms of depression, mania, and psychosis are most often treated by a psychiatrist, often in conjunction with a therapist. The psychiatrist will perform an initial evaluation by asking many questions and taking a thorough history. A preliminary diagnosis and treatment plan will guide what subsequent steps should be taken.

A diagnosis is simply a descriptive term used to identify a cluster of symptoms. The outcome and prognosis is entirely based on a person's individual course. Psychiatrists use a wide variety of medications and other biological treatments to help improve symptoms. In these cases, medication is sometimes crucial to provide needed relief. It relieves the intensity of the symptoms and thereby enables the person suffering from the illness to address his emotional issues in a more rational manner. Medications do have side effects, but untreated mental illness can also dramatically impact one's physical and mental health.

Of course, medications are often not sufficient, as they cannot address all of the factors contributing to one's distress. Religious guidance and practical advice from a *rav* help ground a person who has been spiritually floundering and unable to focus on his relationship with Hashem. Some rabbis have particular expertise in guiding those with mental illness. In addition, there are a variety of health professionals who can provide supportive counseling and psychotherapy.

Therapy is not only for those diagnosed with a mental health condition. Many people in therapy seek help for everyday concerns: relationship problems, child-rearing stress, financial stress, or self-doubt, for example. Some people will resolve their issues through a short course of therapy, while others will need longer-term therapy. Talking to a counselor can help one get at the root of a problem and offer a safe place to discuss conflicting feelings. A good therapist helps one identify self-defeating thoughts, encourages one to make positive changes, and motivates personal growth.

In looking for a therapist, seek one who has ample experience and a professional license. Depending on the problem at hand, one may desire a therapist with a particular treatment orientation. Having a therapist who shares one's Torah values may be of paramount importance, particularly in situations involving struggles with observance and *emunah*. Regardless of the therapist's spiritual perspective, ensure from references that the therapist provides a safe and trustworthy environment.

Many different types of therapies exist, but cognitive behavioral therapy (CBT) and its offshoots have proven to be the most effective. CBT aims to increase an understanding of one's distorted thoughts. These maladaptive thoughts often negatively influence one's behavior and emotions. Changing these destructive cognitions through practical exercises results in improved mood.

The behavioral component involves practicing new behaviors that are more adaptive, thereby leading to improved emotions and better functioning. Other aspects of therapy involve developing a relationship with an empathic person who provides positive feedback and support.

A therapist can also help a person grieve past losses. Therapy may lead to a better understanding of how past traumas contribute to one's current emotional makeup.

Since many factors contribute to sound mental health, other alternative treatments may be very helpful as well, and the various treatments are not mutually exclusive. Gradually incorporating a healthier lifestyle into one's routine can improve one's mental health. Many people will derive much benefit from making their diet more nutritionally sound, incorporating omega-3 fatty acids, whole grains, vegetables, and lean proteins. Many research studies have now shown that regular exercise (roughly thirty minutes five days a week) greatly enhances mental health in addition to physical health. Finally, people with mood disorders in particular gain more stability with regular sleep schedules that ensure adequate and refreshing sleep.

Other alternative treatments may involve the use of herbal remedies, homeopathy, biofeedback, acupuncture, or movement exercises. Since herbal treatments can interact with medications, open communication with all of one's health care providers is crucial.

Utilizing treatments that are safe and that actually relieve suffering should be the main concern. Fear of psychiatric treatment can sometimes lead people to spend much time and money pursuing natural treatments at the expense of reducing suffering through following evidenced-based psychiatric guidelines.

Although finding the right help may require some trial and error, people can and do recover from mental health issues. Obtaining emotional relief can make a big difference in a couple's life together.

Detecting Abuse Early

When Things Aren't Right in Shanah Rishonah

A compilation of information, as told to the author by a certified abuse counselor, as well as women who have been in abusive marriages.

In marriage, there is a range of normal behavior, and there are lines that shouldn't be crossed. There are Jewish women and, occasionally, men being abused knowingly or unknowingly who don't feel they have options or choices. I don't want this book to finish without making it very clear that if, G-d forbid, you suspect that you are being abused, or you know you are, there is help to be obtained and choices to be made.

Abuse can take many forms including: emotional, physical, and verbal abuse. The following will help you identify abusers, potential abusers, and abusive situations.

Certain behaviors define a potentially abusive person. Look out for these risk factors:

- Someone who was emotionally or physically abused as a child

- A person with one or both abusive parents

- A person who has behaved violently toward others

- A person who loses his or her temper frequently

- A person who breaks things when angry

- A person who hits you or your children

If you're not sure what's normal newlywed behavior or whether your spouse's behavior constitutes abuse or potential abuse, ask yourself the following:

- Does he/she have to be in control of everything all the time?

- Does he/she try to isolate you from family and friends?

- Does he/she expect you to spend all your free time with him/her exclusively?

- Does he/she want to know your whereabouts all the time and become angry when you are not available?

- Is he/she very impatient?

- Does he/she become angry if you don't follow his/her advice?

- Does he/she take responsibility for his/her own actions or does he/she always blame you or others for all his/her problems?

- Does he/she deny you any control of finances, or make you report all your spending to him/her?

- Doe he/she put you down? Do you put yourself down in order to please him/her?

- Does he/she appear to have a two-sided personality? Do you feel sometimes as if you're married to a *tzaddik/ tzaddeikes* yet at other times to a monster?

- Does he/she fluctuate between cruelty and smothering kindness?

- Are you afraid of making him/her angry and take great caution not to do so?

- Do you feel you are constantly walking on eggshells?

- Does he/she have unrealistic expectations of you and then put you down for not reaching them?

If the answer is *yes* to many of these questions, you may be in an abusive relationship and seeking help immediately may be your best next step.

If you are afraid of confronting the reality of your situation, you may be in denial. Denial is when one denies a reality because it is safer and/or more comfortable than admitting the reality of the situation. Denial can lead to irreparable deterioration in an abusive relationship.

I have heard women say, "He only hit me once." Once is once too much. A single episode of abuse is not always a reason to terminate a marriage. But it is reason enough to seek counseling.

Abuse is often missed before marriage, especially in the religious world. A person can have many types of relationships before marriage, but the issue that can cause a person to express his abusive side may only surface once a person is married. In second marriages, if a partner was abusive before or was accused of being abusive, be extra careful.

Frequently there is a sequence of abuse:

1. An incident sets off the abuser.

2. This prompts an abusive reaction.

3. The abuser shows contrition, promising it won't happen again or, in some cases, denies that it ever happened at all.

4. The cycle begins again: honeymoon period, buildup of tension, explosion, promises of better behavior, and the cycle repeats itself.

The pattern can be confusing for the abused. If you have any suspicion or a question of whether you are being abused, please go for help. If you do go for help, it is extremely important that you go to a therapist who has experience with, or better yet, specializes in treating abuse. An abusive personality is wired differently than a healthy one, and it is crucial to be guided by an experienced professional.

Never wait for an abusive spouse to change: get help immediately.

In My Experience

———• Malkie Shultz,* survivor of an abusive marriage

The worst advice ever: "Give him more kavod. He'll feel better about himself and then he'll treat you better."

There's one spark of truth in that; theoretically if he felt better about himself, he wouldn't put you down. A person only abuses because deep down he feels horrible about himself.

But it can be a terrible mistake to give more kavod to an abuser. Offering kavod will not make him feel good. It will feed his need to control you and give him an appetite for more. His makeup is not like that of a healthy person. He doesn't feel good when someone gives him kavod. The typical advice of "Treat him like a king and he will treat you like a queen" doesn't apply to abusers. If he gets kavod, it can fill his unhealthy desire for control and possibly lead to putting his wife down even more.

What You Can Do if a Friend Confides in You That She Is Being Abused

One of the sins we enumerate in *vidui* is *"Ya'atznu ra."* Who would purposely give bad advice?

Dr. Abraham J. Twerski explains that *"Ya'atznu ra"* means that we have mistakenly given advice which we thought was helpful, but was indeed extremely harmful. It is like one who tells his friend, "Try this medication, it did wonders for me," without realizing that the medication suggested might be life-threatening to that person. Dr. Twerski adds that unless we understand the problems of spousal abuse, we may unwittingly be giving harmful and dangerous advice to those we care so much about.

If spousal abuse is detected and dealt with early on in the marriage, there may be hope for the survival, and even healing, of the marriage. However, as time goes on and the abuse intensifies, there is significantly less chance for the survival of the marriage. It is therefore crucial that any marriage that has even slight abuse in the relationship get competent help immediately. Allowing the abuse to continue by making believe it doesn't exist, or wishing that it would not exist, is a surefire recipe for disaster.

In concluding this difficult section, I would like to offer some hope. If reading this has made you question your relationship or that of a friend, please remember that most situations have solutions. Summoning the strength to find those solutions is the key. May we all be blessed to find healthy and safe solutions to all of our problems.

Resources: If You Suspect You or Someone Else Is Being Abused

Here are a few options available. New resources are constantly emerging, so consult your Rav and do your own research as well.

1. Shalom Task Force: www.shalomtaskforce.org; Hotline: 888-883-2323

2. Yitti Leibel Helpline: 718-435-7669

3. Ohel Domestic Violence Counseling and Housing Program: 1-800-603-OHEL

4. Confronting Domestic Violence in Israel (www.miklat.org) — provides shelters for women, transitional housing, a hostel for teens, and legal aid (for those living in Israel).

Suggested Reading List

Miriam Adahan. *Sticks and Stones: When Words Are Used as Weapons*. Feldheim Publishers, 1997.

Gila Manolson. *Head to Heart: What to Know before Dating and Marriage*. Targum Press, 2002.

Rabbi Abraham J. Twerski. *The Shame Borne in Silence: Spouse Abuse in the Jewish Community*. Mirkov Publications, 1996.